An Overwhelming Surprise

Hidden in the Final Events

Gerald Lewis Conken

World rights reserved. This book or any portion thereof may not be copied or reproduced in any form or manner whatever, except as provided by law, without the written permission of the publisher, except by a reviewer who may quote brief passages in a review.

The author assumes full responsibility for the accuracy and interpretation of the Ellen White quotations cited in this book. Unless otherwise indicated, all scripture quotations are taken from the King James Version of the Bible.

Copyright © 2021 Gerald Lewis Conken
Copyright © 2021 TEACH Services, Inc.
ISBN-13: 978-1-5725-8504-1 (Paperback)
ISBN-13: 978-1-4796-1412-7 (ePub)
Library of Congress Control Number: 2008924663

Scripture texts labeled (NKJV) are taken from the New King James Version®. Copyright © 1982 by Thomas Nelson. Used by permission. All rights reserved.

Scripture texts labeled (KJV) are taken from the King James Version of the Bible. Public domain.

Contents

Introduction		5
Chapter 1	: The Crisis	9
Chapter 2	: To Save The Planet	25
Chapter 3	: A Voice from the Past	42
Chapter 4	: A Time of Change	47
Chapter 5	: Changing of the Day	54
Chapter 6	: In the Light of Inspiration	67
Chapter 7	: Golden Opportunity or Missed Opportunity	86
Chapter 8	: More Hidden Dangers	99
Chapter 9	: Dawning of a New World	112
Chapter 10	: A Time for Revival	123
Appendix A	: The Sabbath of Creation	138
Appendix B	: The Mark of the Beast	144
Appendix C	: The Spirit of Prophecy	149
Bibliography		154

Introduction

How do you write a book about a crisis that has the potential for turning the lives of all in the world upside down? The prospect of bringing to readers a message of such magnitude can be very intimidating; nonetheless, I cannot remain silent when I see things now taking place in the world, suggesting strongly that the day is at hand.

Events are coming that will bring into question beliefs held dear to the hearts of many devout Christians. How do you tell people that some of what they have sincerely believed all their lives may become the very thing to cause their eternal loss? It will not be a good time when people face the possibility of having their security pulled out from under them. It is with sincere humility that I approach this work. I believe God has allowed me to see through the confusion and smokescreen of current events, to have insight into what is really taking place, where the great deceiver is taking us with events as they transpire.

No, I do not claim to be a prophet. All I am is a searcher for knowledge and understanding regarding events prophesied. Prophecy is not given to confuse the reader but to inform pertaining to future events. Jesus said, "search the scriptures," this does not exclude the prophesies. Again, Jesus said, "And now I have told you before it come to pass, that, when it is come to pass, you might believe" (John 14:29). Not only will it bless us with faith, but also an opportunity to be prepared.

The near future will be one of turmoil. We are nearing the end of this earth's history, and the time allotted to fulfill the commission given us by God. This is a time when events of the most serious nature will be taking place. The consequences of which are of a magnitude not witnessed since creation, and it all appears to be on the near horizon.

It is my prayer that the reader will study this issue carefully before making any judgment as to the validity of this interpretation of current events. For a person not having the historical or instructional background of Seventh-day Adventists, some of the phrases and/or terminology used in this book may be somewhat confusing. For this reason, an Appendix has been included to give a more thorough explanation of some of the more difficult subjects.

This book is written presuming that most readers have knowledge of the elements contained herein. I must stress that the events described here are not limited to Seventh-day Adventists but have a universal application. The Scriptures (Rev.13:3) say that "all the world wondered after the beast." This indicates the world-wide scope of the approaching events.

Satan is setting the stage for the final act in the drama of the ages. A movement will soon involve the whole world in a way that will result in those who are deceived receiving the "mark of the beast." "Be sober, be vigilant; because your adversary the devil, as a roaring lion, walketh about, seeking whom he may devour." "And the dragon was wroth with the woman and went to make war with the remnant of her seed, which keep the commandments of God, and have the testimony of Jesus Christ." "And I fell at his feet to worship him. And he said unto me, See *thou do it* not: I am thy fellow servant, and of thy brethren that have the testimony of Jesus: worship God: for the testimony of Jesus is the spirit of prophecy" (1 Pet. 5:8, Rev. 12:17, Rev. 19:10).

Over one hundred years ago God gave messages to a Christian young lady pertaining to events that would transpire in the last days of this world's history; I will be quoting from these writings, which we believe are a manifestation of a gift of the Spirit, called the Spirit of Prophecy. I could have written this book without references from the Spirit of Prophecy, but these writings penned so long before the events, coming to us from the distant past, contribute an extra degree of understanding. This sneak preview into the near future adds an increased weight of credibility as well. See the Appendix C for an explanation of this phenomenon.

These messages are being fulfilled in the events occurring around us as I write. They have been planned for a long time; Satan has been waiting for the right time to start the ball rolling. That time appears to be here, now!

As Seventh-day Adventists we have been looking for the fulfillment of these prophecies pertaining to the final test, resulting in some receiving the "seal of God," and the remainder receiving the "mark of the beast." This test will be forced upon the entire world in the form of a law enforcing Sunday as a universal Sabbath. Though we may be uncomfortable with the issues associated with Sunday legislation, there is no doubt that the time will come when it is the law of the land. Will we be ready when that time comes? Will the issues be clearly understood? Will we recognize the event as a fulfillment of prophecy, or will we be misled by the manner it is presented to the people?

We know that Satan is working to deceive the very elect; therefore, he is likely to have a movement to enforce a Sunday rest day, by law, so disguised that many will fail to recognize the danger. One such movement is taking the world by storm today.

This book was first published in 2008 under the title *Dawning of the Day: The Coming Crisis Over a Global Sabbath*. Since that time, the world has changed dramatically. One thing has not changed, Satan is going forward at an accelerated pace with his plans to rule the world and receive our worship. At that time, he was making his way in darkness, and now light is beginning to shine on his plans.

This year a pandemic is raging through the power of Satan, by which he is reprogramming the minds of the people. You will find, as you read further, that he is still on track to entangle the world in his deceptions.

The more we know about it, the less likely we will be deceived by what the Spirit of Prophecy says, "will break upon the world as an overwhelming surprise."

Chapter 1

The Crisis

People in the street stand frozen, their eyes riveted on the drama occurring high overhead; expressions of shock grip every face. In my home, I sit spellbound, anchored to the place where much of the next three days are to be consumed. In a moment, the people, horrified, are frantically scrambling for safety to seek shelter from the terror now raining down upon them. The day is September 11, 2001, and the place is New York City.

The horror of that day will stay with all who witnessed the shocking events as they unfolded. We knew we were living in the time of the end, and scenes like that were soon to be commonplace; nonetheless, we were still caught off guard by what had happened.

By witnessing terrible things day after day through the media, we have become somewhat desensitized to the horrors taking place in the world around us. Our little haven of relative peace was, until then, disturbed by comparatively small occurrences of crime and disaster. The "day of the Lord" is approaching, and we in a state of lethargy went on with life as though things would never change. We woke up for a while. More people were going to church than ever before; our political leaders, former rivals, were on TV arm in arm praying and singing together. That didn't last very long either; soon, it was business as usual. I was strongly impressed that the morning of September 11, 2001 marked a change in the degree of protection afforded to this privileged country by our loving Creator.

Then there was Katrina. The monster came to New Orleans, and the city has not yet recovered. There's no need to describe both disasters in detail; the pictures are firmly imprinted on our minds. The problem is that time has a way of blurring the image.

Before long, we find ourselves in the same drowsy state. We take the atrocities for granted. "This is just the world we live in," we say. Yes, it is, but we forget that this is not the way God intended it to be.

The wickedness to which we have become so accustomed, that torments and destroys so many every day, will not end until the day Jesus returns. We must not be blind to the suffering that abounds every day to be lulled again into the same old complacent attitude.

What would it take to wake us up? How much worse does it have to get? Every day we hear of crimes of the most unbelievable character. Lives are lost in accidents by land, sea, and air. War is continually with us, political unrest in every part of the globe, with rebellion and strife between countries and within countries. But, in our little corner of paradise they seem as far away as the moon. We are told that the end and the events surrounding it would come upon the people of the world as an "overwhelming surprise." I can see how that could happen when we are being desensitized little by little.

This world has been the focus of Satan's attack for six thousand years. A dark cloud hangs over this planet as Satan uses the earth to carry forward his attack on the Kingdom of God. As man surrendered his will to the prince of darkness, this world became his playground, and humans his puppets. I, for one, am very tired of what I see taking place in the world around me. I long to see the final act come to a close. What will it take to wake us up?

> But concerning the times and the seasons, brethren, ye have no need that aught be written unto you. For yourselves know perfectly that the day of the Lord so cometh as a thief in the night. When they are saying, Peace and safety, then sudden destruction cometh upon them, as travail upon a woman with child; and they shall in no wise escape. But ye, brethren, are not in darkness, that that day should overtake you as a thief: for ye are all sons of light, and sons of the day: we are not of the night, nor of darkness; so then let us not sleep, as do the rest, but let us watch and be sober. (1 Thess. 5:1–6)

Why are we not all ready and eager to leave this terrible world and all its misery and suffering? The frightening thing is that many of our group will never be ready; the end of all things will come and, when it does, will catch them unprepared. This does not have to be the case. Through the Scriptures and Spirit of Prophecy, God has given us ample warning of coming events. If these resources are utilized prayerfully, there is no reason to be surprised.

We will not be unprepared when the "beast" power of Revelation 13 comes forward with the aid of the "image to the beast," which working together will demand worship from the entire world. None will be permitted to "buy or sell" without compliance, and eventually all who refuse will face the death penalty if they continue to resist. There are predictions of disasters and plagues of the most horrible nature. Many of them will start while Jesus is still acting as our High Priest in the Sanctuary above. I believe we are seeing some of them already.

I want to see things come to an end. I want to look up and see Jesus coming back with all of His angels finally to put an end to sin and suffering, forever. How about you? Now I want to ask you another question. Would you be excited to know that the events pertaining to the establishment of a universal rest day appear to be coming together as you read this? And that the groundwork appears to be on the way to completion? I am writing with the assumption that the reader is aware of Scriptural and Spirit of Prophecy warnings of a movement to institute a universal law-enforced Sabbath.

That "Sabbath," as we believe is to be Sunday, which is the day more commonly observed by Christianity worldwide. A day that is recognized internationally by businesses as a day when many already shut down. A day for which there is no Scriptural basis, no authority other than that of man alone.

Many good Christians today do not realize the day they sincerely observe as the Sabbath is anything less than the Lord's day. I can understand how the information in this book could be troubling. Things have happened in the past concerning the Sabbath that have gone unnoticed by a great deal of honest, sincere Christians. As you read on, much of this will become clearer.

I sincerely believe that God accepts our earnest effort and receives our worship as it is until we are shown that we should do differently. At that time, we are judged on all that we understand.

There is no reason to think that God will not give us advance warning of the direction whence the movement will come. As I write this, we, Seventh-day Adventists, have been preaching an end-time message for nearly two centuries. Yet, up until now there was little indication that the events we have studied and watched for were about to be fulfilled. Nonetheless, time goes on with hardly a hint of their fulfillment.

Those of us who have been members of the church have had to cope with more days upon this earth than we would like. Many become impatient or are distracted by "the cares of this life" or are lured away by the attractions of the world as their patience is tried by the delay. Even more lose the spark they once had for the hope we share of being the generation to witness the final conflict and the glorious return of Jesus.

I can sympathize with those discouraged by the apparent delay; there are probably few in our fellowship who have not at times grown weary. Many have gone to their rest who were expecting to see Jesus come in their day. Looking at the world today, conditions scream for a justice that only the coming of Jesus can supply.

Shakespeare said, "All the world's a stage, And all the men and women merely players" (*As You Like It,* 1529). The stage is being set for the last act in the drama of the ages. We have an opportunity for a sneak peek behind the curtain. Those involved are making last-minute preparations backstage. Much of the groundwork has been laid, and after years of preparation, it now appears ready to open upon an unsuspecting world.

The Scriptures give us an example of being "watchmen" warning of *approaching* danger (Ezek. 33:2–7). In Bible times, most of the people lived in walled cities for protection from enemies and wild animals. Not knowing the day or the hour of the enemy's approach, they were constantly on the watch for the least sign. Eventually, at some unexpected time a watchman, scanning the horizon, caught a glint of light from weapons or armor in the far distance; upon closer observation a faint cloud of dust was observed rising from the location of the flash.

The trumpet sounded, warning the city of approaching danger. Everything changed. All business as usual ceased, those outside the city came in behind the protection of the wall, weapons readied, and supplies were gathered into the city. The early warning made the difference between life and death. Because a faithful watchman was alert, doing his job, a timely warning was given.

Even though time goes endlessly on, someday watchmen will see the first glimmer, the first warning signs of the approaching enemy on our horizon. I believe that time has come. I believe that the first signs are already appearing to show us from which direction the attack will come.

What diabolical plan does Satan have to spring a Sunday law on the unsuspecting public? Over the years, we have heard scenario after scenario speculating on the manner which prophecies concerning the Sunday laws will be fulfilled. There are inherent problems and questions with each one. Such as, how do you convince people of the varied religious and ethnic groups, communist and pagan countries, as well, to honor a Christian "tradition" as they view it? Some believe a financial crisis could convince the world to enforce a Sabbath. There have been scenarios such as a call to bring the nation back to God: books written about asteroid collisions, predictions about Satan impersonating Jesus and deceiving the world. Many non-Christians have their own day of rest and none of these events would be ground enough to enlist their support for a universal Sunday rest day.

There is little doubt that in order to establish a universally accepted day of rest, it would take a crisis of global proportion. The day would not be instituted for a religious purpose, though later in time the law would take on a purely religious character. From the Spirit of Prophecy, we get this insight:

> Here the temperance work, one of the most prominent and important of moral reforms, is often combined with the Sunday movement, and the advocates of the latter represent themselves as laboring to promote the highest interest of society; and those who refuse to unite with them are denounced as the enemies of temperance and reform. But the fact that a movement to establish error

is connected with a work which is in itself good, is not an argument in favor of the error. We may disguise poison by mingling it with wholesome food, but we do not change its nature. On the contrary, it is rendered more dangerous, as it is more likely to be taken unawares. It is one of Satan's devices to combine with falsehood just enough truth to give it plausibility. The leaders of the Sunday movement may advocate reforms which the people need, principles which are in harmony with the Bible,—yet while there is with these a requirement which is contrary to God's law, his servants cannot unite with them. Nothing can justify them in setting aside the commandments of God for the precepts of men. (White, *The Great Controversy,* 1888, 587)

Notice in the above quotation that the movement for a universal Sunday rest day will likely be combined with "temperance work" and "laboring to promote the highest interest of society." The movement "is connected with a work which is in itself good," and they "advocate reforms which the people need, principles which are in harmony with the Bible."

What conditions exist in the world today which need reforming, conditions which involve the whole world and whose movement for its correction is in harmony with the Bible? If a movement is in harmony with the Bible, then it must be of a good character, at least on the surface.

Since it is Satan's purpose to "deceive the very elect" could it not be anticipated that he would choose an avenue for the entrance of the Sunday laws that catches the largest number of God's people off guard? So, what possible crisis would have the potential to inspire *all* the nations to enact a universal day of rest?

There is one such "crisis" today, one that affects all countries alike. Nearly all facets of global society recognize this "crisis." It is accepted equally by religion and science who, by the way, as the result of the "crisis" are working in partnership as never before. This "crisis" has brought together churches and religions the world over like no other in the history of the world. The United Nations is using a great deal of its resources in an effort to combat this "crisis." This "crisis" has brought together under the banner of the "common good" all the mainline churches in this country. Joining them are the New Age and pagan organizations as well along with the international labor unions.

"This issue—more than any other issue—has the potential to overcome race, class, gender, whatever divisions that are plaguing our society," says the late Jean Sindab, speaking at the time from the National Council of Churches. Many prominent world leaders have called it the "greatest crisis the world has ever faced." Former United States Vice President Al Gore on British TV says: "This is by far the most serious crisis civilization has ever faced, it is a genuine planetary emergency, the normal rules of politics should be put aside."

Later in the interview Mr. Gore makes this comment: "The only way in a democracy to get the drastic changes considered by the leaders, whoever they might be, is for the people to be seized of the crisis and demand action." Mr. Gore has plenty of company in his effort to accomplish this goal.

> *The only way in a democracy to get the drastic changes considered by the leaders, whoever they might be, is for the people to be seized of the crisis and demand action.*

You may already have an idea of what this crisis is. There is one and only one that shows signs of being *the one* that meets all the necessary criteria, which could usher in the Sunday laws. This crisis has brought forward a movement to remedy the consequences. That movement is none other than the **environmental movement**, and the crisis: **global warming**.

This movement fits the picture perfectly, and within this movement today, there already is a strong undercurrent for establishing a "Sabbath for the Earth." The interesting thing is that this call is coming from all aspects of society not just the Christian churches.

I'm sure that with this statement many questions will arise; the first to be addressed is what people think of the environmental movement and environmentalists. Before we can take anything said or done by them seriously, we must take a new look at the movement and see just who and what they are.

Many of us see environmentalists as radical "tree huggers." We have seen news clips of Green Peace trying to intercept whaling boats or demonstrators lying on the road in front of bulldozers. These are the radical fringe of the movement who are involved in the early stages of its development.

I have news for you; the environmentalist of today are not the environmentalist of our father's day. Today they could be your federal, state, local government leader, your local pastor or priest, your child's teacher, business leaders, actors, directors, musicians and people from all walks of life. The environmental movement is now mainstream and highly respected in all areas of society.

Another question that arises: what does global warming have to do with the Sabbath, and if there is a Sunday law enacted for the earth, will that be a fulfillment of the prophecies about the mark of the beast? The prophecies pertaining to the Sunday law indicate that it will have an apparently mild and non-religious beginning, but any law enacted to enforce a Sabbath will be an act of worshipping the beast power of Revelation under whose authority it was originally established. It makes no difference what the motive may be.

Many question whether there is actually an environmental crisis and whether global warming is a myth or not. If global warming is a greatly exaggerated hoax, then doesn't that cancel out the likelihood of the issue being used to establish a Sunday law?

The answer: no! The reason I say that is when enough people believe something deeply it is likely that action will result regardless of the truth of the issue; communism is a good example, and the burning of witches in our country, another. How many either remember or have heard of "The War of the Worlds" radio show back in 1938 based on a novel by H.G. Wells? Many believed aliens were invading the world, and mass hysteria resulted. Some people committed suicide. Many believed the story. Was it true? Obviously, until the law is passed, it cannot be stated with 100% certainty that this is the beginning of the movement to establish a Sunday law. Years of study and research have led me to believe, without doubt, that it is. I will proceed to present the evidence; you be the judge. If this scenario plays out as all signs indicate it will, we will each have to face the consequences, and how we respond to the crisis from the very start can determine what the outcome will be. That is why it's so important for each one of us to weigh the evidence and decide for ourselves.

The mountains of scientific articles, as well as firsthand observations, appear to support claims of global climate change that may in future generations have catastrophic results. It is our responsibility as inhabitants of this beautiful world (given to us as a gift from the Creator) to do all we can to preserve it to the best of our ability. The issue I have with efforts to preserve the Earth is what measures are undertaken for its accomplishment. And will the measures taken be contrary to the law of God? It is my firm belief that some measures will not be in harmony with the will of the Creator. Do we not agree that care for the environment is "something needed" and "in itself something good"? I will reveal later how it is also considered a "moral reform."

At the same time, a much wider and deeper understanding of science and technology is needed. If we do not understand the problem, it is unlikely we will be able to fix it. Thus, there is a vital role for both religion and science.

The new direction for the environmental movement began in earnest back in 1990 and took a giant step forward following the circulation of a letter from 32 Nobel laureates and other prominent scientists called an "Open Letter to the Religious Community." The scientists expressed their concern for the direction the environment was headed. There was a sense of urgency. Their appeal to the religions of the world can be summarized by this paragraph from the letter:

As scientists, many of us have had profound experiences of awe and reverence before the universe. We understand that what is regarded as sacred is more likely to be treated with respect. Our planetary home should be so regarded. Efforts to safeguard and cherish the environment need to be infused with a vision of the sacred. At the same time, a much wider and deeper understanding of science and technology is needed. If we do not understand the problem, it is unlikely we will be able to fix it. Thus, there is a vital role for both religion and science. (Sagan, 1990)

The letter was presented in January 1990 at the Global Forum of Spiritual and Parliamentary Leaders Conference in Moscow, Russia.

Present and signing on to the appeal were two hundred and seventy-one, well known spiritual leaders from eighty-three countries: patriarchs, lamas, chief rabbis, cardinals, mullahs, arch bishops, and professors of theology.

As I stated before, the environmental movement of today is not what it started out to be. Not only are religious organizations world-wide deeply involved, but also groups like the United Nations, non-governmental organizations, big business, and educational institutions the world over just to mention a few. The environmental movement has not only enlisted the whole world, but also is unifying the world more than any other in our time. When facing the issues associated with global warming, all barriers are broken down. Religion and science, atheism and Catholicism, paganism and Christianity are all working hand in hand, their differences appear to vanish; all in unity are working for a new supreme goal, "the common good."

Now think for a minute. Forget that the issue we are discussing is global warming. Does not the fact that the world is so absorbed with and united around an issue to the point that all differences are insignificant that old enemies are now standing hand in hand, at least, deserve our attention?

We as a church have been wary in the past of any ecumenical movements that bring together all the churches of the world because by dumping all the churches in a pot and stirring up a religious blend important points of doctrine will have to be discarded leaving a bland mix of godliness without the power (2 Tim. 3:5). It is something that we are unable to join because of the beliefs we hold so dear, which set us apart from the rest of the world. I have news for you, the environmental movement is also the greatest ecumenical movement the world has ever seen, and yet we hear no alarm raised. But since the ecumenical movement is cloaked by another movement that is for the "common good" and "something the people need" the whole issue is totally dismissed or viewed as something entirely harmless.

What is it about global warming that makes it of such concern for the world? What is of such urgency that it could be used by Satan to deceive the world and make them set up a false sabbath and demand that the entire world hold it sacred? I would like to repeat: it does not matter if the problem is real or perceived. What is perceived by enough people will eventually produce action.

We will be focusing on global warming in our discussion of the environmental crisis because, although any pollution of the environment is harmful, pollution of the atmosphere, which causes global warming, has more potential to produce catastrophic results on a global scale.

What are the expected results of uncontrolled global warming? Turn on the television, radio or check the news on the web, pick up a current events magazine and you are likely to come face to face with predictions of gloom and doom from global warming. A special report on global warming called "Be Worried, Be Very Worried" (*Time*, April 3, 2006) is a prime example. There were warnings of temperatures rising worldwide resulting in sea levels rising, droughts with food shortages, flooding in some areas, stronger storms, and with the dry conditions, fierce fires.

The report then outlines how the changes are *already taking place*. Conditions are expected to get worse. With the rise in sea level, large populations will be displaced inland. Farmland will be permanently flooded, some small island nations will require relocation, and it is projected that the poorer countries will receive a disproportionate amount of adverse consequences. Areas prone to tornadoes and hurricanes can expect more and stronger storms; hurricane Katrina was a good example. As temperatures rise, species will be displaced and disease hosts will spread to more temperate climes. Species extinction will accelerate on land and sea in the plant and animal kingdoms alike. Changes in sea temperature will cause coral death, which in turn destroys fish nurseries and, among other factors, will severely reduce sea life, the primary source of income and food for many around the world.

These are only a few of the consequences of global warming. You can see why many people are seriously concerned, and why many are calling on the government to enact laws to correct the situation before it is too late. Many think it may already be too late.

Seventh-day Adventists, along with other Christians, have a tendency to dismiss predictions of natural disaster because prophets have predicted such events before the second coming of Christ. This statement from the prophetic book, *The Great Controversy*, is very representative:

> In accidents and calamities by sea and by land, in great conflagrations, in fierce tornadoes and terrific hailstorms, in tempests, floods, cyclones, tidal waves, and earthquakes, in every place and in a thousand forms, Satan is exercising his power. He sweeps away the ripening harvest, and famine and distress follow. He imparts to the air a deadly taint, and thousands perish by the pestilence. These visitations are to become more and more frequent and disastrous. Destruction will be upon both man and beast. "The earth mourneth and fadeth away...the haughty people...do languish. The earth also is defiled under the inhabitants there- of; because they have transgressed the laws, changed the ordinance, broken the everlasting covenant." (White, *The Great Controversy*, 1911, 589)

Stop for a minute and take a closer look at the paragraph above. As Adventists we are likely very familiar with this statement, but there are things there that I didn't initially notice myself. The statement with the Bible verse is all environmental. Most of it could have been taken from today's newspaper.

Many in the world don't share our outlook of hope for the future. They look for solutions, and a future orchestrated by the hand of mankind, not the hand of God. When their livelihood or safety is at risk, they look to any source they can for an answer. This situation is no different. Changes are coming, and some of them will greatly affect the people of God. Regardless of what we believe, scientific consensus and momentum are on the side of the environmentalist.

An excellent example of how the world views the global warming crisis is illustrated by an article I read very recently. The article is from MSNBC News Services (2006).

A leading U.S. climate researcher says the world has a 10-year window of opportunity to take decisive action on global warming and avert catastrophe.

NASA scientist James Hansen, widely considered the doyen of American climate researchers, said governments must adopt an alternative scenario to keep carbon dioxide emission growth in check and limit the increase in global temperatures to 1 degree Celsius (1.8 degrees Fahrenheit).

> "I think we have a very brief window of opportunity to deal with climate change…no longer than a decade, at the most," Hansen said Wednesday at the Climate Change Research Conference in California's state capital. If the world continues with a 'business as usual' scenario, Hansen said, temperatures will rise by 2 to 3 degrees Celsius (3.6 to 7.2 degrees F) and "we will be producing a different planet."
>
> On that warmer planet, ice sheets would melt quickly, causing a rise in sea levels that would put most of Manhattan under water. The world would see more prolonged droughts and heat waves, powerful hurricanes in new areas and the likely extinction of 50 percent of species. (MSNBC News Service, September 14, 2006)

Other articles speak of water and food crises as mountain glaciers melt and climate is altered with the accompanying droughts and floods. Still others speak of major rivers that dry up hundreds of miles before they reach the oceans, large lakes that are shrinking, others that are dying, and the list goes on, too numerous to include here.

On February 2, 2007, the Intergovernmental Panel on Climate Change (IPCC) released their Summary to the Climate Change 2007 report. That report was the most powerful argument concerning the reality of global warming ever released.

On that date the Associated Press filed a report; the following quotation is from that report:

> Environmental campaigners urged the United States and other industrial nations to significantly cut their emissions of greenhouse gases in response to the long-awaited report by Intergovernmental Panel on Climate Change. "It is critical that we look at this report...as a moment where the focus of attention will shift from whether climate change is linked to human activity, whether the science is sufficient, to what on earth are we going to do about it," said Achim Steiner, the executive director of the U.N. Environment Program. (Crittendon, 2007)

This report is expected to bring on board those governments that have been reluctant to join the rest of the world in working to control global warming (including the U.S.). Those who have resisted have done so because of risk to their economies. However, recent studies have shown that it would be more expensive to ignore global warming than to take measures to correct the problem.

On February 2, 2007, the environmental movement turned a corner. Until that day the emphasis was on proving that global warming was real. From that day on, it has been what we can do about global warming. Since that day, politicians, policy makers, talk show hosts, all in the public arena, are talking about that issue in particular. We should watch carefully what solutions are recommended. Already it is becoming unacceptable to speak out against environmental science or efforts to correct global warming.

Major changes are coming to our world spurred on by the global warming crisis. It isn't a matter of if there will be changes, but what the changes will be. We can be assured of one thing: the world is soon to be a very different place. There will undoubtedly be lifestyle changes, and changes in the way we do business. Demands are coming from all facets of society for laws to halt, and if possible, reverse the direction the environment is going; and they want action to start now.

The bottom line is this: the people of the world are frightened about what is taking place *now* with the environment. Scientists, world leaders, and others of influence are demanding that the United States take the lead in reversing the buildup of greenhouse gases that cause global warming. One reason for asking our nation to take the lead is that though we are a small minority of the world's population, we produce 25% of the greenhouse gasses spewed into the atmosphere every day. Another reason is that we are the world's leader especially in the area of technology. The U.S. would need to be a part of any effort; otherwise, it would be unlikely to succeed.

If man had been obedient to the commands of God from the beginning—keeping the Sabbath—we would not have the environmental crisis we have today.

Seventh-day Adventists have been preaching the observance of the true, original Sabbath for over a century and a half. We haven't been doing so just to be legalists as many have accused but because we believe that what God sanctifies remains so for eternity as he did with the Sabbath: "Thus the heavens and the earth were finished, and all the host of them. And on the seventh day God ended his work which he had made; and he rested on the seventh day from all his work which he had made. And God blessed the seventh day and sanctified it: because that in it he had rested from all his work which God created and made" (Gen. 2:1–3).

By way of the environmental movement, man appears to be very interested in and concerned for the creation that occurred on the first six days, while disregarding that of the last day, the Sabbath. The Sabbath was just as much a part of creation as mankind. This was centuries before the establishment of Judaism, and God said that the Sabbath was created for man (Mark 2:27).

If man had been obedient to the commands of God from the beginning—keeping the Sabbath—we would not have the environmental crisis we have today. Remembering the Sabbath would have helped man to remember his Creator and would have kept him in harmony with the rest of the created world. There is more later in the text and in Appendix A relating to the change of the Sabbath and the consequences of its enforcement.

Amid the quietness of a drought stricken landscape or the shriek of the hurricane above the roar of the flood can be heard a multitude of voices calling for action—fearful voices, cries for their children, and what kind of world they will have to endure? The calls for action are growing with every passing moment and each new heat wave. The calls for action are loud; eventually those voices will fall on receptive ears. The laws will come; changes to our way of life will result. Some of the changes may well have monumental consequences. A glimpse into the future may give us insight into what lies ahead.

CHAPTER 2

To Save the Planet

People starving, and others driven from their homes by rising seas, cities destroyed by tremendous storms; the earth is facing the greatest crisis in modern history, and the people are looking for solutions. How can they save the earth from present disaster and future generations from the heavy burden of even worse consequences? These are concerns worthy of all the attention they seem to be receiving. But how did this interpretation of prophecy that these solutions will eventually result in a Sunday law or "Sabbath for the Earth" come together?

The process of discovery began in the late '90s. At the time, my wife and I were discussing (as do many of us looking for the final events to unfold) what could possibly serve to bring in the Sunday laws—what we as a church should look for, as the last prophetic event to take place before Jesus returns. Signs of the times strongly suggested that we were approaching the time just prior to the enacting of those laws. Few of the prophecies of the end had not taken place.

I felt certain that God would not let something of such importance transpire without giving us some advance warning. The Spirit of Prophecy is vague on the issue of the Sunday laws. There is little in it to indicate what issue would bring them about. I use the plural because the Spirit of Prophecy does tell of Sunday *laws*.

As we discussed the issue with prayer and study, we were impressed that the only event at the present time that would have the universal appeal to prompt all nations to adopt a Sunday law had to be the environmental crisis.

The "crisis" at that time was not as widely accepted. There were more people denying it than supporting. But, I began my investigation anyway. Something had to come along and lend itself to the establishment of a Sunday law, and there was nothing more promising than this.

My search began on the internet. I started by researching everything I could about the environmental crisis. I was sure that if this were the issue to usher in the Sunday laws, there would be some indication in the articles and books written on the subject. I wasn't expecting it to be an easy search because if we were correct Satan would do his best to conceal the fact.

At first the articles were from scientists who were just beginning to be vocal on the issue. Scientific studies were scarce then, but many scientists were making computer projections indicating that if CO_2 levels continued to climb a greenhouse effect could cause the atmosphere to warm leading to climate disruption and a wide array of undesirable effects.

The thing that interested me most was their call for the entire world to unite behind efforts to correct the problem. The idea of the world uniting caught my attention. Whatever the cause, we know that the world would have to eventually unite because "all the world wondered after the beast" (Rev. 13:3).

My research limped along for several years. The information gathered increasingly supported our contention that this was the issue that would bring on the Sunday law crisis, but concrete evidence was lacking.

As I continued to research the subject, I chose to do a web search on the topic of environment and religion; if Sunday laws were to result from this issue, surely the churches would be involved. The most impressive discovery was a website for the National Religious Partnership for the Environment (NRPE). At that time, I had no idea of any religious involvement in the environmental movement. I discovered not only that religions are involved, but also that involvement was far greater than anticipated. For instance, in the case of the NRPE there are four groups in the partnership: the U.S. Conference of Catholic Bishops, the National Council of Churches, the Coalition on Environment and Jewish Life, the Evangelical Environmental Network.

According to a booklet published by a joint effort of the Interfaith Partnership for the Environment (IPE) and the United Nations Environmental Programme (UNEP) entitled *Earth and Faith-A Book of Reflection for Action*, the NRPE in 2000 represented "a broad coalition of 135,000 churches." When I first discovered the NRPE we were going through a time in which we moved twice within a relatively short time. You know how moving can disrupt everything, so during that time the research was understandably put on the back burner.

After the last move in 2003, we were in the public library at our new home. I was scanning the videos looking for something with a nature theme when I came upon a video with a breaching whale on the cover. The title was *Keeping the Earth, Religious and Scientific Perspectives on the Environment* (1996). Immediately my attention peaked. Curiously, I turned it over, and to my surprise the producers were the National Religious Partnership for the Environment and the Union of Concerned Scientists. Suddenly I was back in the investigative mode. We took the video home and without hesitation inserted it into the VCR. Immediately the booming voice of James Earl Jones was heard, "In the beginning God created the Heaven and the earth," while beautiful scenes of nature streamed on the TV set. Soon the scene changed to the Cathedral of St. John the Divine in New York City. Down the aisles of the church strolled a procession of animals and plants. A voice was heard saying "what was out there now belongs in here." Then the narrator returned to reading the scriptural account of the creation week.

Scientists and theologians alternated with Mr. Jones, describing the deplorable condition of the environment reciting how the earth is our home regardless of our understanding of its origin, and how we must do all we can to restore and protect "our home."

The story line departs for a minute from the creation week: the narrator is now reading the account of the flood.

Corresponding scenes flowed across the screen. Calvin DeWitt, Director of the Au Sable institute said

> The first endangered species act is where Noah is asked by the Creator to take two of every kind and preserve their

lineages, and it's interesting that the cost of this endangered species act is immense. Noah spends perhaps something like one hundred years, immense resources, very valuable wood, a great deal of time and perhaps the most devastating of all to most of us would be the derision that one would get if one would spend a hundred years building a very large boat on absolutely dry land. But the result is, he is the one who is faithful in preserving the species and preserving their line, and the rest of the people perished from the Earth. (1996)

The narration of the creation week continues, my anticipation climbs as Mr. Jones finishes with day six. What will be said about the Sabbath and the environment? Would this video—produced by a joint effort of science and religion—support our theory of an environmentally inspired Sunday law?

The narration momentarily leaves the subject of the creation week. Voices talk of how man is occupying and damaging every inch of space available on planet earth; we see a picture from space of North America at night clearly outlined by the lights visible in the darkness. And then one more comment, this time by Mr. Paul Gorman, Director of the NRPE, "In a certain sense we conduct a continuing conversation with God as we move through the natural world. If that's true, somehow every act which destroys a species, circumscribes our conversation with our Creator. The destruction of a species of God's creation is metaphorically like tearing a page out of Scripture" (1996).

There is a pause, and the scene which had moments earlier been of large, crowded, noisy, brightly lit cities is now one of a quiet neighborhood with a stark absence of any activity whatsoever. The booming voice of James Earl Jones returns, "Thus the heavens and the earth were finished, so God blessed the seventh day and hallowed it, because on it God rested from all the work done in creation" (1996).

At this point I am shaking my head, how unbelievable that such a video was produced by a partnership including a scientific organization. Science has traditionally been at odds with religion, especially the Bible, but here it is. A beautiful program filled almost entirely with Scripture.

Calvin DeWitt speaks again, "One of the things we are asked to do in the Scriptures is not relentlessly press creation. That is done through the teaching of the Sabbath. The Sabbath not only for human beings, but a Sabbath for the land" (1996). Wow!

There it is! A partnership of science and religion are advocating a "Sabbath for the land."

Mr. DeWitt continues; "If we relentlessly press the land then what we do is to interfere with the capacity of the land to restore and rejuvenate itself, if we do that, we begin to erode the very home upon which human life depends" (1996).

There are more comments from the scientists about destroying the earth and then Mr. DeWitt speaks again; "If we are really honest about our own lives we have not only violated the Sabbath for the earth, but we also have violated the Sabbath for ourselves. We have gotten on what we call the treadmill, the rat race; we spend a lot of time racing around, and there is a necessary first step, and that is, we have to scale back in some of our frenzied activity to the point where we can reflect on who we are, why we are here, and where we are going" (1996).

I think we can agree on that, can't we? We have been telling the world that for over a hundred and fifty years. We have been opposed by the same people who now think it is a good thing since there is an environmental crisis, and to do so may help the situation.

What do the scientists on the video think of the idea? Jean Lubehenco, president of the American Association for the Advancement of Science comments next: "I think there is a growing movement that is accepting this moral responsibility, and saying, 'things aren't right, this is not the way it's supposed to be, what do we do about it'? That's where I see a partnership between science and religion, serving a very powerful, very important role" (1996).

Now my theory of the environmental crisis possibly serving to bring in the Sunday law is much less a theory and more of a probability. Here are very prominent scientists and religious leaders advocating a "Sabbath for the earth" and doing so in a very impressive way. As I write this, it is important to note that this week the very scientific organization that produced this video was testifying before Congress on global warming.

A little question still remained. Were they really advocating a weekly Sabbath as a solution for the crisis, and were they thinking of enforcing it by law? While pondering that question, I purchased one of the videos for my own records, and while on the phone with the Union of Concerned Scientists, I discovered that there was a discussion guide that accompanied the video. I was anxious to see what they said about the issue of the Sabbath. I discovered that one purpose for the video was to play it before groups—at church, clubs, and public gatherings.

When it came, my question was answered. Under the heading, "Activities for After Showing the Video," it reads like this:

> 8. Discuss the concept of the Sabbath. Ask students:
>
> Do you think that the idea of a Sabbath is valuable to us today? Why or why not?
>
> What kind of lifestyle changes might occur if everyone were to observe a weekly Sabbath? Can you imagine a universal day of rest?
>
> If you were to declare a weekly Sabbath for the people or a periodic Sabbath for all the land, what are some of the laws you would put into effect? (Union of Concerned Scientists, 1996)

Did you catch the significant phrases: "lifestyle changes," "if everyone were to observe a weekly Sabbath," "universal rest day," "what are some of the laws you would put into effect"? I can answer the last one: Sunday laws, universal Sunday laws! Is there any doubt what day people would choose to "declare" for a universal Sabbath if they were to enact one? This video and discussion guide were produced by two very influential and powerful parties. Should not this at least quicken our pulse just a little? All this and a great deal more going on right under our noses, and we were for the most part oblivious to it all.

The Spirit of Prophecy gives insight that is very appropriate, at this point in time: "While men are sleeping, Satan is actively arranging matters so that the Lord's people may not have mercy or justice. The Sunday movement is now making its way in darkness. The leaders are concealing the true issue, and many who unite in the movement do not themselves see whither the undercurrent is tending" (White, *Early Writings,* 1882, 452).

One reason we have not been aware of these happenings may be because we already have an idea of how the Sunday laws will arrive, and this doesn't fit the picture. Could we have been looking in the wrong direction all these years? Looking in one direction while the enemy was quietly approaching from another. In prophecy, there is nothing clear about the factors leading to Sunday laws. What is said has to be studied carefully or a misunderstanding may occur.

What I have presented thus far is just "the tip of the iceberg." Who else is talking about a Sabbath for the Earth? Concerning the movement making its way in darkness while we slept: *since 1984 there has already been an annual Sabbath for the Earth celebrated throughout the world.*

> *While men are sleeping, Satan is actively arranging matters so that the Lord's people may not have mercy or justice. The Sunday movement is now making its way in darkness.*

The United Nations Environmental Program established one at that time to focus attention on the need to preserve the earth. The Environmental Sabbath is the *Sunday* closest to Earth Day. If there is any question as to the possibility that a Sabbath law could be established on the premise of helping the environment, this should remove any doubt. One Sunday a year is already set aside for the purpose of protecting the earth. Already the stage is set. How difficult would it be to expand that idea and back it up with a law? As we saw earlier, some are already thinking about it, the only thing lacking is the proper atmosphere and right time. Those conditions are nearer realization with each setting sun.

Shortly after the institution of the Environmental Sabbath program, the U.N. through the Interfaith Partnership for the Environment distributed thousands of packets of information to congregations across the U.S. and Canada with materials and instructions on how to conduct environmental Sabbath services. Take for instance this opening statement from some of that literature a prayer regarding the environmental Sabbath:

> We who have lost our sense and our senses—our touch, our smell, our vision of who we are, we who frantically force and press all things, without rest for body or Spirit, hurting our earth and injuring ourselves; we call a halt. We want to rest. We need to rest and allow the earth to rest. We need to reflect and to rediscover the mystery that lives in us, that is the ground of every unique expression of life, the source of the fascination that calls all things to communion. We declare a Sabbath, a space of quiet; for simply being and for recovering the forgotten truths for learning how to live again. Amen. (United Nations, 1990)

How long before someone decides "if a Sabbath for the earth is good one time a year, wouldn't it be even better every week"?

Now, so far, we have a powerful partnership between science and religion. Following the efforts of the United Nations, both are supporting and in the case of the U.N. establishing a Sabbath for the Earth. What other organizations are supporting a movement for the establishment of a Sabbath for the Earth? Let's read some quotations and let them speak for themselves:

> In the last ten years there has been a growing interfaith response to the environmental challenges we face. This was evidenced by the 1992 UN Earth Summit in Rio that was not only attended by more than 170 heads of state, but leaders of every spiritual denomination. It was very powerful to join together and share our *common concerns and goals*, which are reflected in the Agenda 21 Action Plan and the UN's Environmental Sabbath program.

These efforts were furthered in this country with the creation of the National Religious Partnership for the Environment, composed of leading Roman Catholic, Jewish, evangelical Christian, and mainline Protestant organizations. Each faith tradition networks with the others and has developed its own umbrella organization. For example, I serve on the National Board of the Jewish one, the Coalition on the Environment and Jewish Life.

Clearly, there is a new message emerging from the pulpit that *ecology must be joined with theology* and day-to-day life in our religious institutions and community. Priests, pastors, rabbis and other spiritual leaders around the country are working with their congregants to be responsible stewards of Creation and address global climate change. (Gips 2001, emphasis added)

Whereas humanity is sometimes described as the "crown of creation," it is more faithful to the Genesis account of the seventh day to see the Sabbath itself, as the crown. Certainly, the Sabbath was intended to be a pause to allow the earth time to recover from human use for its resources, but the theme is richer than that. The weekly observance of the Sabbath is an anticipation of that state of equilibrium which God intends shall be the crown of creation. The rhythm of Sabbath days and Sabbath years reclaims time from a mere succession of passing moments and gives life a shape which flows from a recognition that creation was not brought into being to serve any transient human purpose but to be material for the praise and glory of the Creator.

"Today creation 'wears man's smudge and shares man's smell;' it is 'seared with trade; bleared, smeared with toil' (Gerard, "God's Grandeur"), knowing no respite from the demands of human beings addicted to a cult of 'more. The Sabbath needs to be reinvigorated, not as a reversion to some fantasy search for 'Victorian values,' but as a feast of redemption and an anticipation of the ecological harmony and sustainable equilibrium of Christ's kingdom." (Chartres, 2001)

The "Sabbath needs to be reinvigorated." This coming from an influential Anglican Bishop. Another article calls for a "Sabbath for the Earth," and in so doing echoes words in the Spirit of Prophecy. The editor of *Worldviews, Religion, and the Environment*, Richard C. Foltz, writes, "'the environmental crisis is merely a symptom—albeit a highly dramatic one of a deeper spiritual crisis.' Seeing people and issues in terms of black or white—and segregating accordingly, is perhaps the deepest moral scar. Like the Civil Rights Movement, a successful environmental movement requires deep spiritual underpinnings. *At best, faith communities can only limp along if people of faith do not demand a Sabbath for the earth*. Likewise, the largely secular environmental movement will be hobbled if it does not embrace *a religious or spiritual dimension*" (Jill D. Rios, from an award-winning article for the Southern Environmental Law Center entitled, "Back to the Garden: Cultivating Environmental Advocacy in the Christian South").

Does this statement ring a bell? Maybe this quote will sound familiar: "To secure popularity and patronage, legislators will yield to the demand for Sunday laws" (White, *Last Day Events*, 132.4). This prophecy gives a valuable clue to how Sunday laws will be enacted. Unlike previously held opinions that the laws will come in as the result of demonic intervention, this statement implies that they will result from public pressure. It also implies that the impetus to enact such laws will come from the people, and that politicians will need to be convinced or persuaded. In reference to the above prophecy, let's look at a statement made by Al Gore in an interview with Jonathan Freedman on British TV May 26, 2006. The context of the comment is the global warming crisis and how to get politicians to act. Here is what he has to say:

> We have to change the minds of the people in the United States, and elsewhere in the world. We have to put the truth before them in a clear and persuasive and undeniable way, so that the people being informed of the truth of our situation, will then demand of the politicians and in the process give them the permission they need to have some

courage to make the dramatic changes that will solve the crisis.

There's that "demand" word again. Let's look at some more quotations.

After a careful reading of the Old Testament passages that speak about the importance of a Sabbath—a moment of rest—one must reconsider the issue. Jurgen Moltman speaks of an ecological ethic that reclaims the importance of the Sabbath for the Earth. Old Testament teaching clearly instructs the importance of allowing the land to rest. Where most industrial policy fails is on its intention of pulling resources without any regard to a Sabbath rest for the land. If we continue to pull the resources from this earth without allowing it, the God given right of rest, this living organism we call earth might begin to fight back. If not given its Sabbath by humanity, there is the possibility it will take it any way it can achieve it.

R. Mitch Randall, President, Christians for Change, in an article entitled, "Ecological Responsibility" said this "living organism... might begin to fight back" (2005).

Sounds a little like "the gaia hypotheses" has made its way into the philosophy of this writer. We will see later how much pagan philosophy has infiltrated into even the church viewpoint of the environment. In this context read this statement from the Unplug America organization:

> The "Unplug America—Give Mother Earth a Rest Day" campaign was introduced in 1992 by Indigenous Peoples to invite all people to show our love and respect for our Mother Earth and all the sacred Life Circles by challenging unhealthy patterns of consumption and the continued production of poisons that destroy our environment.
>
> October 13 is a day to "Unplug," turn off the TV and radio, shut off the taps, take a walk and leave the fossil-fuel burning vehicle at home. It's only one day but it's the first step towards restoring our land and resources- to reflect on

> how much we actually consume—individually, nationally and globally—a starting to act for future generations.
>
> No one is saying to go freeze in the dark. It has to do with taking only what you need and being a responsible human being. We need to take action and save our resources. Our future depends on it.

The appeal above sounds a lot like a call to be temperate or to exercise "temperance," as in: "Here the temperance work, one of the most prominent and important of moral reforms, is often combined with the Sunday movement. The leaders of the Sunday movement may advocate reforms which the people need" (White, *The Great Controversy,* 1888, 587).

From an "Invitation to Churches and Ecumenical Groups in Western Europe," the World Council of Churches and World Alliance of Reformed Churches commented:

> According to Lev. 25 and other texts the Jubilee vision includes: Sabbath for the Earth...This means that the Bible points to the root causes and gives divine demands to avoid ecological destruction, impoverishment, and debt in the first place. Yet since injustices do happen, the Bible also gives rules and regulations so that equality and right relationships can be restored periodically—not only once in every generation. For many aspects of healing and restitution are applied every seventh year [Sabbath year; cf.e.g. Deut. 15] or every third year [Deut.14], indeed every week [Sabbath, Lev. 23:3]

Matthew Sleeth of AlterNet commented on the condition of the environment and the lack of cooperation between evangelicals and environmentalists

> So why do we care who gets to save the planet? Should we not be rejoicing instead that so many are working hard to save it?

To begin with, here is a Christian tradition that all can benefit from: celebrating the Sabbath. The fourth commandment "Honor the Sabbath," is a mental health prescription that has served humans well for millennia. If Americans did no work, no shopping, no driving one day a week, we would instantly produce fewer greenhouse gases, use billions of gallons less fuel, and be closer to sanity and to God. The Sabbath is God's gift to man, 52 times a year. (2005)

Dr. Sleeth is a Methodist M.D. who gave up an ER practice to "focus on the most pressing health issue of all times: Earth Care" (2005).

These writers all have something in common, they all have a deep concern for the environment. They all see a bleak future for the Earth unless something is done. And they all see a Sabbath for the Earth as one solution.

If enough support for an environmental Sabbath develops, what day will be chosen for that Sabbath? Unfortunately, there are not enough people keeping the original Sabbath for that day to be chosen. The day most of the world accepts as a Sabbath is undoubtedly Sunday. Even in countries where Christianity is a minority, Sunday is a day when business comes to a standstill because so much of the western business world does so. Why would there be enough support to enact a Sunday law for the Earth? Let's look at a quotation from the book, *Divine Rest for Human Restlessness: A Theological Study of the Good News of the Sabbath for Today*, by Samuele Bacchiocchi:

> Suppose we were to ask modern science; What benefits would accrue to human beings and their environment from observing the Sabbath according to traditional biblical guidelines? Such observance would involve shutting down for the duration of the Sabbath factories, shops and places of entertainment. It would mean stopping industrial machines as well as the millions of automobiles on the highways with the exception of those needed for social services.

The result would be a cessation on the Sabbath in the flow of pollution into our atmosphere which in some of our metropolises has become a toxic smog: A scientific report on New York City's atmosphere indicates that the average person on the street of that city inhales toxic fumes equivalent to 38 cigarettes per day [Robert and Leona Rienow, *Moment in the Sun,* 1967, pp. 141ff.]. (1998)

I'm sure it's much worse now. This one day with a greatly reduced demand for energy (power plants are one of the largest sources of air pollution) and much less exhaust produced would give the air a greatly needed break, a chance to "breathe" so to speak. One day in seven with reduced greenhouse gas production would lower the overall average by a significant amount. A country attempting to fulfill reduction requirements such as those set up by the Kyoto Accord could use this means to reduce the overall level of greenhouse gases without causing a great strain on their economy.

There would be benefits in the area of energy dependence as well. Many believe that major lifestyle changes are necessary now to avoid catastrophic climate changes later. Studies show that the majority of people would be willing to make those lifestyle changes to correct the problem of global warming.

The reasoning just illustrated appears to be a very practical approach to the problems the energy and environmental crises present. Therefore, what would be wrong if a Sunday law were enacted under these premises? Nothing would be wrong in complying with a law calling for us to rest on a day we don't hold sacred as our Sabbath. It would be different though if because of our resting on the first day of the week, we didn't keep the true Sabbath holy. The time will come when man is forced by law to observe Sunday as a holy day, forcing us to worship on that day. That would change the situation completely.

Being forced to stop work on another day in addition to our Sabbath would pose a financial hardship for many. But, the greatest problem with nations setting aside a day as the Sabbath would be in honoring a false Sabbath established on no other authority than that of the Roman Catholic Church. Bible scholars of various denominations for centuries believed this organization to be the beast power of Revelation of which it is said: "all the world wondered after the beast" (Rev.13:3) and received Her mark.

God established a Sabbath day and "hallowed it" (Gen. 2:3). When He did, He made a sacred day that no man could change. The Scriptures tell us that God "never changes" (reference), so what He has made sacred stays sacred. God had a plan for the preservation of the Earth and the spirituality of man. Had it been kept or *remembered* as the commandment admonishes, we would not have the problems we now have. Also, as we are reminded by environmentalists from many of the churches who have made the movement a "moral" issue, God commanded the celebration of a Jubilee every seven years in which the Earth was allowed to rest for a year.

God knows what we and the Earth need and has made provision for those needs. Trying to correct the deplorable condition of things on this world by counterfeiting what God has already done and doing so on a day adjacent to the original is nothing but open rebellion against the law of God, which calls for us to "remember the Sabbath day" (the seventh-day Sabbath). And yes, it would be a fulfillment of the prophecy pointing forward to a time when the *"earth and them which dwell therein"* (Rev. 13:12) would worship the beast.

The above text points to a time when the Earth is made to rest on the false Sabbath. Why do you suppose the Earth was said to worship the beast? To receive the mark of the beast one would have to observe a rest day enforced by law in opposition to the Sabbath of the Lord. Will a Sabbath enacted (by the beast power) to cause the Earth to rest on a day other than the true Sabbath cause the earth to worship the beast? How many of us will be deceived? How many will see it as a good thing as something *"which the people need"*?

I am not saying that any of the above-quoted people are intentionally working to create a legislated Sabbath to force everyone to worship on that day. Many times, men set out to achieve a certain outcome by enacting laws which eventually create hardship and persecution for a segment of the population.

A prime example being the actual enforcement of Sunday observance in the time of Constantine the Great. The book *The Great Controversy* gives this accurate, historically proven account:

> Royal edicts sustained by secular power, were the steps by which the pagan festival attained its position of honor in the Christian Royal edicts, general councils, and church ordinances world. The first public measure enforcing Sunday observance was the law enacted by Constantine [A.D. 321.]. This edict required townspeople to rest on "the venerable day of the sun," but permitted countrymen to continue their agricultural pursuits. Though virtually a heathen statute, it was enforced by the emperor after his nominal acceptance of Christianity.
>
> The royal mandate not proving a sufficient substitute for divine authority, Eusebius, a bishop who sought the favor of princes, and who was the special friend and flatterer of Constantine, advanced the claim that Christ had transferred the Sabbath to Sunday. Not a single testimony of the Scriptures was produced in proof of the new doctrine. Eusebius himself unwittingly acknowledges its falsity, and points to the real authors of the change. "All things," he says, "whatsoever that it was duty to do on the Sabbath, these we have transferred to the Lord's day." But the Sunday argument, groundless as it was, served to embolden men in trampling upon the Sabbath of the Lord. All who desired to be honored by the world accepted the popular festival.
>
> As the papacy became firmly established, the work of Sunday exaltation was continued. For a time, the people engaged in agricultural labor when not attending church, and the seventh day was still regarded as the Sabbath. But steadily a change was affected. Those in holy office were forbidden to pass judgment in any civil controversy on the Sunday. Soon after, all persons, of whatever rank, were commanded to refrain from common labor, on pain of a fine for freemen, and stripes in the case of servants.

Later it was decreed, that rich men should be punished with the loss of half of their estates; and finally, that if still obstinate they should be made slaves. The lower classes were to suffer perpetual banishment. (White, *The Great Controversy,* 1888, 574)

It has happened before, and it also involved the elements involved in the environmental Sabbath movement today, such as: the civil powers and the Papacy as we will see in the following chapters. We have just read statements from important individuals suggesting a Sabbath for the Earth as a solution to the environmental crisis. These are by no means the only people making such recommendations. If I were to print all that I have collected over the years, this book would have nothing in it but those quotes.

I believe these alone are enough that any student of Bible prophecy would be willing to acknowledge the importance of the direction they were heading. Those of us who have been looking for these events to transpire cannot help but be excited as we see where it is going.

Chapter 3

A Voice from the Past

Before we look at recent, exciting events taking place pertaining to a Sunday law, let's look into an important and really serious question; why does it matter? This question is more likely to be raised by those who claim no religious affiliation; those who do not worship or believe in a God.

Many pay little attention to what transpires in the world concerning religious matters. They are happy with their lives, satisfied to go about their lives without any concern for controversial matters. None of those issues affect them, or do they?

The crisis of the last days involve the mark of the beast (See Appendix B). In the book of Revelation, we see that everyone will either have the "seal of God," or "the mark of the beast." The Bible clearly describes what is to happen to those who have the mark. Our decisions, in the near future, will determine what group we will be in, whether or not we believe in God, have a form of godliness without the power, just go along with the act that constitutes worshipping the beast, or whether we obey the true God and worship Him. There will be only two groups, no in-between, either we worship God and keep His commandments, or we reject His commandments and follow the will of man.

In those days there, will be no peace or safety. The earth will be in turmoil; by choosing to worship the beast, people will be under total control of Satan who plunges the world into the worst time of trouble there has ever been. At that time, if we are on board with those who are following man instead of God, we will be worshipping the beast who gets his power from Satan. The only people who have peace and safety will be those who worship God and keep His commandments.

As we continue to trace the course of the Sabbath for the Earth movement, we need to see clearly that the issue of a forced false-Sabbath is an issue that concerns everyone. In the final crisis, there will be no neutral observers. Let us now look at the most recent events in the "Sabbath for the Earth" movement.

The twenty first century, so far, has seen a continued focus on the environment, with a growing concern that time was running out for us to halt global warming before it reached a point of no return. Not only have the predictions been serious but the results of global warming are already beginning to be felt around the world.

Heat waves are scorching the cities and drying out forested areas, leading to tremendous wildfires and deaths in the cities due to the heat. Storms are more powerful and frequent. Ice in the polar regions that had been around for centuries is melting at an increasing rate causing an accelerated rise in sea levels. The world is becoming more and more united in efforts to halt the warming. Voices calling out for action are reaching a crescendo along with fear for what the future holds.

In 2015, one voice began to rise above most others; that was the voice of Pope Francis. The Pope took his name from the famous priest, Francis of Assisi, who was known for his care of nature. He is rapidly being recognized as the spokesperson for the environmental movement because of his outspoken stance on protection of the earth.

On May 24, 2015, Pope Francis released his famous Encyclical on the environment, entitled *Laudato Si'* which contained solutions for how to address the environmental crisis. I include here some quotes from the Encyclical:

> On Sunday, our participation in the Eucharist has special importance. Sunday, like the Jewish Sabbath, is meant to be a day which heals our relationships with God, with ourselves, with others and with the world. Sunday is the day of the Resurrection, the "first day" of the new creation, whose first fruits are the Lord's risen humanity, the pledge of the final transfiguration of all created reality.

It also proclaims, "man's eternal rest in God." ...The law of weekly rest forbade work on the seventh day 'so that your ox and your donkey may have rest, and the son of your maidservant, and the stranger, may be refreshed' (*Ex* 23:12). Rest opens our eyes to the larger picture and gives us renewed sensitivity to the rights of others. And so, the day of rest, centered on the Eucharist, sheds it light on the whole week, and motivates us to greater concern for nature and the poor. (2015, 237)

This clearly expresses what the Pope sees as a viable solution to the environmental crisis. Notice how he has linked care for the poor along with keeping Sunday as a day of rest. It is interesting to note that his Encyclical has received praise from people in all walks of life, professors, politicians, religious leaders from nearly all denominations, and most importantly leaders in the environmental movement.

> *And so, the day of rest, centered on the Eucharist, sheds it light on the whole week, and motivates us to greater concern for nature and the poor.*

Following the release of his Encyclical voices of approval echoed around the globe from the U.N. Secretary General to theologians, professors of higher education, scientists, and politicians, all praising it as a wonderful approach to solving the environmental crisis.

Why are we so concerned with the activity of the Pope? Well, as the quote at the end of the previous chapter reveals, the Pope in A. D. 321 was instrumental in not only changing the Sabbath from Saturday to Sunday (see Appendix A) but was also responsible for enacting a law enforcing Sunday observance. It was the Bishop of Rome, then, responsible for the act. We are certain that it will be someone in the same position that will be active in instituting one in the future.

The consequences of such an act will plunge the world into a much greater crisis than global warming. Therefore, whatever the Pope does now could have serious ramifications later on. More on this will be revealed in later chapters and in the Appendix. The wisest man on earth once said, "what has been will be again" (Eccl. 1:9).

Move ahead four months, the scene is a highway leading to the capital building in Washington, DC. The streets are lined with thousands of cheering, ecstatic people. The reception was fit for a king as the Pope mobile made its way slowly to the capital building where thousands more were anxiously waiting.

Moments later the Pope was introduced to a joint session of congress making his way slowly down the aisle waving to those on each side, apparently pleased by the reception. After the thunderous applause subsided, the robed Pontiff stepped to the microphone and began his historic speech to the leaders of our nation.

Over much of the next hour he described the condition of our world—instructing the distinguished audience as to their responsibility for correcting the deplorable state of things. As expected, he did not fail to include the state of the environment in his comments, and our need to protect it.

After his speech he was escorted by the Speaker of the House of Representatives to a balcony where he stood very reminiscent of the balcony at the Vatican where he blesses the crowd in St. Peters Square. In similar fashion he blesses the excited as thousands gathered below.

The next day the Pope was visiting the headquarters of the United Nations in New York giving a similar speech to the representatives of most of the nations of the world, and he received the same favorable response. I think it would be safe to say "the deadly wound" is healed.

Wake up, children of God! In scripture what followed the healing of the "deadly wound"? "All the world wondered after the beast" (See Revelation 13). The beast and the image to the beast receive the worship of the whole world. It isn't a coincident that the Pope is deeply into the environment and is on the scene at this time in history.

In both speeches much of the material presented was taken from his encyclical on the environment. The unofficial leader of the environmental movement has solidified his position among the nations of the world. Looking back to the quote at the end of the last chapter and then to the next chapter, we will see why this is so important.

The remainder of the first two decades of the 21st century continued along the same path. Storms creating havoc; enormous wildfires destroyed thousands of acres and thousands of homes; and entire towns were destroyed.

To illustrate how prominent the movement has become, a young Swedish teenager named Greta Thunberg led hundreds of thousands of youth and adults in environmental protest marches in cities around the world. Greta because of her popularity was invited to address a meeting of the U.N. summit on climate change where she scolded lawmakers because of their inaction. As a result of her activism, she was chosen as *Time* magazines person of the year. As a result of her and other's actions, global warming has been given a new face and another voice.

Chapter 4

A Time of Change

Near the end of 2019, an interesting development was taking place. Pope Francis, the "voice of the environmental movement," issued a surprising invitation. He invited leaders from all areas of society, business, sports, government, education, the arts, etc., to meet with him at the Vatican on May 14th, 2020, to take part in a global alliance called, "Reinventing the Global Compact on Education."

The meeting is proposed as a focus on education of the children, but as he states in his invitation, there is another dimension as well. Notice how it reads: "An alliance, in other words, between the earth's inhabitants and our 'common home', which we are bound to care for and respect. An alliance that generates peace, justice, and hospitality among all peoples of the human family, as well as dialogue between religions."

What does that have to do with children? Reeducation is necessary before changes. The focus of the alliance is to reeducate the people to accept other ideas and lifestyles. An interesting fact to remember is that in the first line of the invitation he referenced his Encyclical, *Laudato Si'*, which reveals the hidden purpose for the alliance: "In my Encyclical, *Laudato Si'*, I invited everyone to cooperate in caring for our common home and to confront together the challenges that we face. Now, a few years later, I renew my invitation to dialogue on how we are shaping the future of our planet and the need to employ the talents of all, since all change requires an educational process aimed at developing a new universal solidarity and a more welcoming society" (2020).

It is well that he refers to his Encyclical since much of the invitation is taken from that document and it is my guess that it will be the guidebook for the meeting. If the Encyclical is prominent in the meeting and the call for keeping Sunday central to the document, would it not be possible that a Sabbath for the Earth could come up in the process?

As 2020 arrived scientists continued to predict cataclysmic changes. Greta traveled the world focusing attention on the future of young people in a damaged world, and the Pope's meeting drew closer, all pointing to the prospects of something important taking place.

Then, the pandemic arrived, and the entire world turned upside down. Most governments of the world enacted measures to combat the spread of the virus. The most common measure was to quarantine the people by stay at home orders. Businesses and factories and all non-essential services were put on hold. The entire world was essentially paralyzed.

Suddenly people were talking about the environmental movement taking a back seat because of the economy. Governments were preparing for a depression and combating global warming was not high on the agenda.

Then, weeks into the pandemic the picture began to change; evidence began to come out about an unusual finding by satellite observers. It became apparent that the levels of greenhouse gasses in the air over China were dropping dramatically due to the shutdowns and stay at home orders, Scientists using satellite observation were noticing the same results in other heavily populated areas of the world as well.

People noticed the air becoming clearer where normally masks had to be worn to prevent an unhealthy reaction to the air pollution. Water became clearer and the sky became a darker blue.

Scientists began to promote the idea that some good may come from the pandemic. Articles began appearing about the possibility of continuing the benefits of the shutdown after a return to normal. People were likening the shutdown to a Sabbath. Some saying the earth is finally getting a rest.

Look at this article from Geoff Bansen, Digital Meteorologist:
With everyday life coming to an abrupt halt, our planet

has been given a chance to breathe. In an effort to contain the spread of the pandemic, many factories have been shuttered. Planes sit idly on runways as travelers cancel flights and airlines slash service. More and more of us are working from home, cutting traffic to a bare minimum.

The global shutdown caused by the virus has inadvertently become the biggest experiment ever in the reduction of greenhouse gases. Many environmentalists see this as an opportunity to make significant strides in preventing serious outcomes from climate change.

People have taken some pretty drastic measures in recent weeks given the situation at hand. While these changes have been extreme, they show that the world has the ability to make adjustments—adjustments that can help to limit negative effects on our climate.

It also shows that, perhaps, humans are capable of under standing the threat of something that cannot be seen.

The hope of many climatologists is that if even half of the population continues parts of this energy-friendly quarantine lifestyle once everything reverts to normal—teleworking, consolidating trips, limiting food waste—that we could see measurable, positive results. (2020)

The global shutdown caused by the virus has inadvertently become the biggest experiment ever in the reduction of greenhouse gases. Many environmentalists see this as an opportunity to make significant strides in preventing serious outcomes from climate change.

Planners are working to find ways to prevent the pollution from going back to the high levels recorded before the pandemic, or worse. What about the Educational Alliance?

This article from the *Catholic News Agency* tells what is planned for the 5th anniversary year of the Pope's environmental Encyclical. It is entitled "Vatican to Mark 5th Anniversary of *Laudato Si'* with Year-Long Celebration."

It noted that the environmental encyclical's anniversary also falls in the midst of the global coronavirus outbreak, saying "*Laudato Si*'s message is just as prophetic today as it was in 2015."

"The encyclical can indeed provide the moral and spiritual compass for the journey to create a more caring, fraternal, peaceful and sustainable world," the Vatican department said.

The initiatives undertaken in partnership with other groups have "a clear emphasis on 'ecological conversion' in 'action,'" it continued.

In 2021 the dicastery will start institutions such as families, dioceses, schools, and universities on a seven-year program to work toward integral ecology through the lens of *Laudato Si'*.

The Vatican events, "Reinventing the Global Educational Alliance" and the "Economy of Francesco," which were due to have taken place this spring and have been postponed to the fall, are now also classified under the anniversary year celebrations, according to the schedule (Brockhous, 2020).

With the changes taking place in the world, it would be reasonable to be somewhat uncertain as to what is going to happen. Events appeared to be progressing rapidly toward a Sabbath for the Earth, now the focus seems to be on the pandemic and the economy. How does the prospect for an Earth Sabbath look now? Stop and think for a minute. Remember that Satanic agencies are deeply involved in anything that can be used to further Satan's plans.

He does not work in only one manner, but instead he takes advantage of any opportunity or event that serves his purposes. He has been working under cover for centuries marshaling his forces and putting everything in place for his final attack.

So, we have a pandemic and an environmental crisis at the same time. Isn't it possible for him to use both to accomplish his goals? The pandemic was his work just as the environmental crisis is. Why did he choose to bring it out now? Think of it. If you were to plan and arrange things so that you could institute a global Sabbath, could you find a better scenario?

During the pandemic most of the world was in shut down. People were quarantined to their homes; non-essential businesses were shut down or operated by drive through. Many workers were doing their jobs from home. For most people their normal routines were discarded.

How does this further his plans? Think about it for a minute. Before the pandemic, how difficult would it have been to convince the whole world to honor a day of rest for the Earth?

Before the Covid-19 virus the world was on a fast roller coaster ride of unrestrained growth. Economies were flourishing. The skies were full of airliners transporting millions of people to every inch of the globe, for fun and profit.

Then the world came to an abrupt halt. While the pandemic raged, the skies cleared which did not go unnoticed by those who previously had been crying for measures to accomplish just that. Some began to wish the benefits could remain after the pandemic. Read what Leah D. Schade, Assistant Professor of Preaching and Worship at Lexington Theological Seminary in Kentucky, says in her article entitled, "When Earth Demands Sabbath: Learning from the Coronavirus Pandemic."

One tiny virus is attacking us, slowing us down, and even stopping us in our tracks. So as Earth is finally getting the sabbath it needs, we can use this time to rethink our relationship with the planet going forward.

> One tiny virus is attacking us, slowing us down, and even stopping us in our tracks. So as Earth is finally getting the sabbath it needs, we can use this time to rethink our relationship with the planet going forward. We can make different choices that protect both Earth and our

neighbors. Hopefully this pandemic will show us that not only are we capable of making different choices, but that we must.

Rather than being forced into an emergency stop, we can return to the ancient biblical wisdom of planned, regular, and complete rest for ourselves and God's Creation. Is it so bad to have stores close at 9 p.m.? Would it be unbearable to have one day a week when everyone –workers and consumers alike—gets a day to rest? Can we understand the prudence of leaving forests and natural lands alone to live as God designed? (2020)

What is happening to those millions who are sitting at home during the pandemic? They are having their lives reset. Like an electronic device that is acting up and needs a reset. What better time to introduce a one day a week break to save the earth and prevent worse pandemics in the future? The people have been on a "sabbath" for months; they have been at home with their families and away from business, sports, and other crowded activities. It would seem a small sacrifice to change it to just one day a week. After all they are beginning to like having more time with their families.

This pandemic is the perfect time to introduce changes in lifestyles. People are ready to press for a Sabbath for the Earth, and people will use the threat of worse pandemics, the suffering of the poor, the loss of species, worse storms, coastal flooding, and many other threatening disasters to drive for acceptance of their goal.

The wisest man ever to live on this earth gave us a warning that applies well at this point. He said, "what has been done will be done again, there is nothing new under the sun" (Eccles. 1:9, NIV). Man has in the past enforced a Sabbath by civil law. They thought their actions were for a good purpose. As we have previously read, those who enact Sunday laws will think they are doing something "the people need." Will we recognize it when it comes? Will we be ready?

Once begun, the law will undergo a gradual transformation. What is initially instituted to serve a common—an attempt to correct global warming—will eventually be hijacked by religious powers in an attempt to appease an angry God. At this time, the "beast" power of Revelation will step in with its previous history of Sabbath enforcement, and it will take the world captive. As we continue, we will see how those changes take place and explore other dangers involved with this movement.

CHAPTER 5

Changing of the Day

Tension mounts as the hero and heroine piece together clues in the form of symbols on a map, while the bad guys are rapidly approaching. The duo works frantically. With no time to spare, a picture begins to take shape revealing the information they need to continue their quest for the treasure, and they escape seconds before the enemy arrives. This is a scene from a popular movie. It illustrates well the manner and urgency with which one needs to decipher the prophecies concerning the last days especially those concerning the Sunday laws. These prophesies deal with the most important issues since the first advent of Jesus: the final test to determine who will be ready, and the second coming of Jesus. The object of understanding last-day events is on a level with the work of John the Baptist just prior to the first advent of Jesus. By having a correct understanding of end-times prophecies, we can participate in the process of preparing a people for His return.

How does something as innocent and apparently harmless as observing a Sunday Sabbath change so dramatically until it becomes a test that will decide the destiny of all mankind? There are ample clues throughout the inspired writings; we only need to know how the information is to be assembled and interpreted. We can do that only with the aid of the Holy Spirit and an attitude of prayer. One other important ingredient needed is a willingness to accept and incorporate what the Spirit reveals into our thinking and our daily lives even if it is different from what we have previously understood.

Information in the Scriptures and the Spirit of Prophecy is often scattered about in bits and pieces much like a jigsaw puzzle on a tabletop. At first, we may be overwhelmed as nothing makes any sense. The pieces look as though they could fit together in many varied arrangements. Sometimes we connect pieces together and later find that we had made a mistake. No matter how much it looks right, they were just not meant to be combined in that fashion. Finally, when pieces are united in proper sequence, they begin to create semi-recognizable forms. These groups help in properly placing other previously confusing parts of the puzzle until finally a picture takes shape, and what was once a confusing disarray, now makes perfect sense.

This is nothing more pronounced than in the material pertaining the establishment and development of the Sunday laws. The Spirit of Prophecy provides information on this subject in scattered bits and pieces throughout various books and articles. To make sense of the information we will need to carefully study the quotations in their proper context. It is also necessary to compare the material with scripture and history. (To understand more about the Spirit of Prophecy, see Appendix C.)

There are ways to avoid confusion regarding the Scriptures. One is to let the scriptures give their own interpretation (2 Pet. 1:20). Another is to compare scripture with scripture (Isa. 28:10–13). In prophecy, symbols are frequently used, and these should also be explained by Scripture. It is also important to remember that Biblical understanding does not necessarily increase with the number of years a person spends in the educational system. In other words, a person does not need to be a *scholar* in order to understand the Bible. While even the simple can understand (1 Cor. 2:14), the Bible can be confusing to even the most highly educated if they are not consecrated enough to listen to the Holy Spirit's prompting.

According to the Spirit of Prophecy, the establishment of a Sunday law will follow a certain order. This is the sequence that I have found in my studies. It all begins when a crisis develops that will become the catalyst for its enactment. I firmly believe that the environmental crisis will be that catalyst; therefore, much of the following scenario will be based on that assumption. In no way am I trying to prophesy the events about to take place, but I am merely illustrating how it fits into the prophecies that we do have.

Starting as a relatively mild law it soon takes on a new character. Once started, the following sequence is prophesied:

1—To secure popularity and patronage, legislators will yield to *the demand for a Sunday law.* By the decree enforcing the institution of the papacy in violation of the law of God our nation will disconnect herself fully from righteousness...As the approach of the Roman armies was a sign to the disciples of the impending destruction of Jerusalem, so may this apostasy be a sign to us that the limit of God's forbearance is reached. (White, *Early Writings,* 1882, 451)

> *1—To secure popularity and patronage, legislators will yield to the demand for a Sunday law. By the decree enforcing the institution of the papacy in violation of the law of God our nation will disconnect herself fully from righteousness.*

This statement is clearly speaking of the United States and establishes the fact that the process for the enactment of a Sunday law begins with the people through our democratic processes. The initial law will apparently be mild in nature and will likely have little in the way of religious characteristics. It will appear to be "something the people need," and "in harmony with the Bible." Following the example of the United States, the remainder of the world will enact Sunday laws as well.

2—As America, the land of religious liberty, shall unite with the papacy in forcing the conscience and compelling men to honor the false sabbath, the people of every country on the globe will be led to follow her example. (White, *Testimonies for the Church, vol. 6,* 1901, 18)

"The Sabbath question is to be the issue in the great final conflict in *which all the world* will act a part" (White, *Testimonies for the Church, vol. 6,* 1901, 352).

"Foreign nations will follow the example of the United States. Though she leads out, yet the same crisis will come upon our people in all parts of the world" (White, *Testimonies for the Church, vol. 6,* 1901, 395).

Following the first enactment, drastic changes will begin to take place in this country which will have profound influence on the future course of the Sunday laws.

3—When our nation, in its legislative councils, shall enact laws to bind the consciences of men in regard to their religious privileges, enforcing Sunday observance, and bringing oppressive power to bear against those who keep the seventh-day Sabbath, the law of God will, to all intents and purposes, be made void in our land, and national apostasy will be followed by national ruin. (White, *SDA Bible Commentary, vol. 7A,* 1970, 977)

2—As America, the land of religious liberty, shall unite with the papacy in forcing the conscience and compelling men to honor the false sabbath, the people of every country on the globe will be led to follow her example.

"And he (the beast representing the US) exerciseth all the power of the first beast before him, and causeth the earth <u>and</u> them which dwell therein to worship the first beast, whose deadly wound was healed" (Rev. 13:12). Isn't it interesting how the book of Revelation could describe the time when the world is coaxed into keeping the first beast's Sabbath (illustrated as worshiping the beast and, also, how the *earth* is also shown to "worship the first beast"? A law that mandates Sunday as sacred constitutes the mark of the beast. I have read this verse time and again in my studies, and only through the environmental connection did its significance become apparent.

> The day of God is right upon us. The world has converted the church. Both are in harmony and are acting on a shortsighted policy. Protestants will work upon the rulers of the land to make laws to restore the lost ascendancy of the man of sin, who sits in the temple of God, showing himself that he is God. The Roman Catholic principles will be taken under the care and protection of the state. This national apostasy will speedily be followed by national ruin. The protest of Bible truth will be no longer tolerated by those who have not made the law of God their rule of action. Then will the voice be heard from the graves of martyrs, represented by the souls which John saw slain for the word of God and the testimony of Jesus Christ which they held; then the prayer will ascend from every true child of God, "It is time for thee, Lord, to work, for they have made void thy law." (White, *Review and Herald,* June 15, 1897)

Notice the frequent reference to *laws*–in the plural. The reason will become apparent as we continue.

Immediately following the initial establishment of a Sunday law, God will no longer protect this country from the assault of Satan due to the neglect of the law of God and the support of a false Sabbath. Terrible times will follow which will have marked results and will greatly affect the future course of the Sunday laws.

> By the decree enforcing the institution of the papacy in violation of the law of God, our nation will disconnect herself fully from righteousness. When Protestantism shall stretch her hand across the gulf to grasp the hand of the Roman power, when she shall reach over the abyss to clasp hands with spiritualism, when, under the influence of this threefold union, our country shall repudiate every principle of its Constitution as a Protestant and republican government, and shall make provision for the propagation

of papal falsehoods and delusions, then we may know that the time has come for the marvelous working of Satan and that the end is near. (White, *Maranatha*, 1976, 216)

And the nations were angry, and *thy wrath is come*, and the time of the dead, that they should be judged, and that thou shouldest give reward unto thy servants the prophets, and to the saints, and them that fear thy name, small and great; and shouldest destroy them which destroy the earth. (Rev. 11:18)

4—Satan puts his interpretation upon events, and they think, as he would have them, that the calamities which fill the land are a result of Sunday breaking. *Thinking to appease the wrath of God* these influential men make *laws enforcing* Sunday observance. (White, *Maranatha*, 1976, 176)

As conditions get worse, people will attempt to correct the problem, not by turning back in obedience to God, but to more severe Sunday laws.

> As the movement for Sunday enforcement becomes *more bold and decided*, the law will be invoked against commandment keepers. They will be threatened with fines and imprisonment, and some will be offered positions of influence, and other rewards and advantages, as inducements to renounce their faith. But their steadfast answer is: 'Show us from the word of God our error.'[...] Those who are arraigned before the courts make a strong vindication of the truth, and some who hear them are led to take their stand to keep all the commandments of God. Thus, light will be brought before thousands who otherwise would know nothing of these truths. (White, *Maranatha*, 1976, 186)

When it becomes "more bold and decided," the law will become more religious in nature, which would be Satan's plan all along. We are facing a cunning foe who knows how to manipulate the human race to accomplish exactly what he desires. It is his plan to establish a Sunday law for the Earth using a cause the whole world can easily support. When in place, Satan can arrange things in such a way that it would not be difficult to convert it into a religious law. This is especially the case with the religious slant the environmental movement and the world's religious community is developing. The process continues. With every new act of rebellion on man's part, the situation worsens leading to even more rebellion much like the experience of Pharaoh in response to the plagues on Egypt.

> 5—As men depart further and further from God, Satan is permitted to have power over the children of disobedience. He hurls destruction among men. There is calamity by land and sea. Property and life are destroyed by fire and flood. Satan resolves to charge this upon those who refuse to bow to the idol which he has set up. His agents point to Seventh-day Adventists as the cause of the trouble. "These people stand out in defiance of law," they say, "They desecrate Sunday. Were they compelled to obey the law for Sunday observance, there would be a cessation of these terrible judgments." (White, *Maranatha*, 1976, 216)

When the world is united in support of the "Sabbath for the Earth," those who speak out against it will be slandered, mocked, and ridiculed. Those united will be deceived and will argue that the law is necessary to save the Earth.

> Our land is in jeopardy. The time is drawing on when its legislators shall so abjure the principles of Protestantism as to give countenance to Romish apostasy. The people for whom God has so marvelously wrought, strengthening them to throw off the galling yoke of popery, will, by a national act, give vigor to the corrupt faith of Rome, and thus arouse the tyranny which only waits for a touch to start again into cruelty and despotism. *With rapid steps are we already approaching this period.* (White, *The Signs of the Times,* July 4, 1899, emphasis added)

Satan puts his interpretation upon events, and they [leading men] think, as he would have them, that the calamities which fill the land are a result of Sunday-breaking. Thinking to appease the wrath of God, these influential men make *laws enforcing Sunday observance.* They think that by exalting this false rest-day *higher, and still higher,* compelling obedience to the Sunday law, the spurious sabbath, they are doing God service. Those who honor God by observing the true Sabbath are looked upon as disloyal to God, when it is really those who thus regard them who are themselves disloyal, because they are trampling underfoot the Sabbath originated in Eden. (White, *Maranatha,* 1976, 176)

6—No one has yet received the mark of the beast. The testing time has not yet come. There are true Christians in every church, not excepting the Roman Catholic communion. None are condemned until they have had the light and have seen the obligation of the fourth commandment. But when the decree shall go forth enforcing the counterfeit sabbath, and the loud cry of the third angel shall warn men against the worship of the beast and his image, the line will be clearly drawn between the false and the true. Then those who still continue in transgression will receive the mark of the beast.

The change of the Sabbath is a sign or mark of the authority of the Romish Church. Those who, understanding the claims of the fourth commandment, choose to observe the false sabbath *in the place of the true*, are thereby paying homage to that power by which alone it is commanded. With rapid steps we are approaching this period. When Protestant churches shall unite with the secular power to sustain a false religion, for opposing which their ancestors endured the fiercest persecution, then will the papal sabbath be enforced by the combined authority of church and state. *There will be a national apostasy, which will end only in national ruin.* (White, *Signs of the Times,* November 8, 1899)

The mark of the beast is the papal sabbath, which has been accepted by the world in the place of the day of God's appointment. (White, *Signs of the Times,* November 8, 1899)

The so-called Christian world is to be the theater of great and decisive actions. Men in authority will enact laws controlling the conscience, after the example of the papacy. Babylon will make all nations drink of the wine of the wrath of her fornication. Every nation will be involved. Of this time John the Revelator declares: (Rev. 18:3–7; 17:13, 14), "These have one mind." <u>There will be a universal bond of union, one great harmony, a confederacy of Satan's forces</u>. "And shall give their power and strength unto the beast." Thus is manifested the same arbitrary, oppressive power against religious liberty—freedom to worship God according to the dictates of conscience—as was manifested by the papacy, when in the past it persecuted those who dared to refuse to conform with the religious rites and ceremonies of Romanism. (White, *Maranatha,* 1976, 188)

We have already seen how united the world has become around the issue of the environment, working toward a set of laws and regulations that would create a condition to be seen by many as the "ushering in of the long expected millennium":

The line of distinction between professed Christians and the ungodly is now hardly distinguishable. Church members love what the world loves and are ready to join with them, and Satan determines to unite them in one body and thus strengthen his cause by sweeping all into the ranks of spiritualism. Papists, who boast of miracles as a certain sign of the true church, will be readily deceived by this wonder-working power; and Protestants, having cast away the shield of truth, will also be deluded. *Papists, Protestants, and worldlings will alike accept the form of godliness without the power, and they will see in this union a grand movement for the conversion of the world and the ushering in of the long expected millennium.* (White 1911, *The Great Controversy,* 588, emphasis added)

The issues at this time will not only be the exaltation of a false Sabbath, but the disregard of the true Sabbath. With the establishment and enforcement of a Sunday Sabbath, pressure will be exerted to force men to transfer the work they would normally do on the first day of the week to the seventh, the Sabbath day of creation. This isn't surprising given the fact that the goal of Satan, from before the creation of the world, has been to undermine the sacred law of God. No other area has he been as successful, as with the fourth commandment.

> I saw that God will in a wonderful manner preserve his people through the time of trouble. As Jesus poured out his soul in agony in the garden, they will earnestly cry and agonize day and night for deliverance. The decree will go forth that they must disregard the Sabbath of the fourth commandment, and honor the first day, or lose their lives; but they will not yield, and trample under their feet the Sabbath of the Lord and honor an institution of Papacy. (White, *The Review and Herald,* 1862)
>
> 7—Fearful is the issue to which the world is to be brought. The powers of earth, uniting to war against the commandments of God, will decree that all, 'both small and great, rich and poor, free and bond,' shall conform to the customs of the church by the observance of the false sabbath. All who refuse compliance will be visited with civil penalties, and it will finally be declared that they are deserving of death. On the other hand, the law of God enjoining the Creator's rest-day demands obedience and threatens wrath against all who transgress its precepts.
>
> With the issue thus clearly brought before him, whosoever shall trample upon God's law to obey a human enactment, receives the mark of the beast; he accepts the sign of allegiance to the power which he chooses to obey instead of God. The warning from Heaven is: "If any man worship the

beast and his image, and receive his mark in his forehead, or in his hand, the same shall drink of the wine of the wrath of God, which is poured out without mixture into the cup of his indignation." (White, *The Great Controversy*, 1911, 604–606)

After all have had a chance to decide for themselves whom they will worship, the declaration from God—as recorded in the book of Revelation—will be given, and all destinies will be sealed with their probation ended.

> And he saith unto me, Seal not the sayings of the prophecy of this book: for the time is at hand. He that is unjust, let him be unjust still: and he which is filthy, let him be filthy still: and he that is righteous, let him be righteous still: and he that is holy, let him be holy still. (Rev. 2:10–11)
>
> 8—Even though the destinies of all will have been decided, Satan's work is not finished. He still has one last plan to "deceive the very elect." Satan sees that he is about to lose his case. He cannot sweep in the whole world. He makes one last desperate effort to overcome the faithful by deception. He does this in impersonating Christ. He clothes himself with the garments of royalty which have been accurately described in the vision of John. He has power to do this. He will appear to his deluded followers as Christ coming the second time. The Christian world will follow Satan because they "received not the love of the truth but had pleasure in unrighteousness [transgression of the law]" [2. Thess. 2:11, 12].
>
> He proclaims himself Christ, and he is believed to be Christ, a beautiful, majestic being clothed with majesty and, with soft voice and pleasant words, with glory unsurpassed by anything their mortal eyes had yet beheld. Then his deceived, deluded followers set up a shout of victory, "Christ has come the second time! Christ has come! He has lifted up His hands just as He did when He was upon the earth, and blessed us." (White, *Last Day Events*, 1992, 164)

(We will see in the next chapter that this "last desperate effort" will occur after the close of probation during the time of the plagues.)

From this sequence we can see a law that begins as apparently benign. It is "something the people need," "for the common good," and the preservation of our environment. Gradually it changes, manipulated by the church into a religious law culminating in the persecution of those who choose to keep the true Sabbath of the Commandments.

This is the manner in which Satan has worked throughout his reign. Starting something under a disguise of being wholesome or useful with no sign of danger is like a pond covered with thin ice and snow. The danger is not apparent until the victim is in serious trouble.

There is serious danger in this movement for the people of God. A danger that it will not be recognized, and that it will not be seen as a fulfillment of prophecy. If we are unmoved by the initial stages of this Sunday law and go about our lives as if there were nothing to be concerned about, then we could be like the proverbial frog on the stove in a pot of cold water with the heat increasing gradually. The frog is not aware of what is taking place until it's too late. The issue is not just a matter of days to be chosen at man's discretion. The issue is whether we will obey the law of God. As with Israel when in bondage to Egypt, the prerequisite for deliverance is obedience.

The end of the earth, and of time as we know it, is right before us. What an awesome time this is. Just the prospect of that which is approaching is very humbling. Many throughout time have dreamed of seeing this period of earth's history. People in our church have hoped to be alive when it happened. Should we get excited? I believe enough has been done already to lay the groundwork for a "Sabbath for the earth", that yes, we should get excited; we have the tremendous privilege of living at this time. It is not only a privilege, but also a great responsibility. If this is the beginning of the end, we have much to do to prepare. In addition to the preparation we also have a great work to do.

We must remember, the Spirit of Prophecy tells us that the final movements will be rapid. All the warnings and advice given us in years past by God's prophets are of the utmost importance at this time. We have heard them all at one time or another. We tire of them because nothing appears to ever change, and things go on as they have for years. That seems to be changing now. Those words can now take on a new life. What we have been expecting for so long now appears to be on our doorstep. Yes, it is ok to get excited! We must get excited!

CHAPTER 6

In The Light of Inspiration

One cannot deny that the prospects are gigantic. If this information is correct, what a profound impact it can have on our lives! The things we have considered most important would now drop to the bottom of the list, and spiritual matters take on a new urgency. Our value system would require an overhaul. Trivial matters will become just what they are supposed to be, trivial.

There is not an Adventist alive who would not like to believe this is true. We have waited for so long to see a manifestation of the final events in the conflict of the ages, but it would be normal to have a degree of skepticism. There have been false alarms in the past like one large one just prior to the birth of our church.

The Sunday laws that we have expected to arrive at some future time appear to be just around the corner riding in on the coattails of environmental laws. Along with skepticism about the environmental movement, some may have problems accepting this scenario because it is nothing like the picture often drawn of the end times. This is no reason to toss out the whole matter. Isn't this the way Satan has been known to work? Choose a means that will catch as many as possible off guard. Remember what the Bible and the Spirit of Prophecy said that the final events will burst upon the world as an "overwhelming surprise"? How can something be a surprise unless it comes unexpectedly?

When I first presented this interpretation to fellow church members, a friend of mine expressed a concern that it wasn't compatible with the Spirit of Prophecy account of end-time events. This inspired me to study deeper. If I was right about this interpretation, there should be evidence enough to answer any objections relating to the Spirit of Prophecy. The material presented in this chapter is the result of that study.

The concern expressed by my friend was a belief that many in our church, including myself at one time, have held for years. That scenario, which has so influenced our understanding of last-day events, is of Satan impersonating the coming of Christ and claiming to have changed the Sabbath from Saturday to Sunday. We have expected a crisis to precede his coming, such as a natural disaster, terrorist attack, monetary crisis, which he declares will be resolved if all the world would keep holy the false Sabbath.

> *Satan sees that he is about to lose his case. He cannot sweep in the whole world. He makes one last desperate effort to overcome the faithful by deception. He does this in personating Christ.*

All that is in this statement is correct. The Spirit of Prophecy does say that Satan will impersonate Christ and will claim to have changed the Sabbath from the seventh day to the first. He will also encourage everyone to keep the false Sabbath. The only problem is the place in time. What is the context? In real estate they say it's all about "location, location, location." In prophecy, this one in particular, it's all about context, context, context.

We will come back to this concern later, but first let's look at some other factors. There are several inherent problems with this interpretation: First, how does a being who resembles Jesus convince all the religious and ethnic groups worldwide to keep a Christian "tradition" when Christ's own people didn't accept Him when He lived among them? Satan is a talented impostor, but he cannot be more convincing than Jesus Himself. He was still rejected.

Another concern about Satan's impersonation of Christ can be found in these statements from the Spirit of Prophecy:

> Satan sees that he is about to lose his case. He cannot sweep in the whole world. He makes one last desperate effort to overcome the *faithful* by deception. He does this in personating Christ...Then his deceived, deluded followers set up a shout of victory, "Christ has come the second time! Christ has come! He has lifted up His hands just as He did when He was upon the earth and blessed us...
>
> The saints look on with amazement. Will they also be deceived? Will they worship Satan? Angels of God are about them. A clear, firm, musical voice is heard, "Look up." *There was one object before the praying ones—the final and eternal salvation of their souls.* This object was before them constantly—that immortal life was promised to those who endure unto the end. Oh, how earnest and fervent had been their desires. *The judgment and eternity were in view.* Their eyes by faith were fixed on the blazing throne, before which the white-robed ones were to stand. This restrained them from the indulgence of sin....
>
> One effort more, and then Satan's last device is employed. He hears the unceasing cry for Christ to come, for Christ to deliver them. This last strategy is to personate Christ and *make them think their prayers are answered*." (White, *Last Day Events,* 1992, 165)

I have placed emphasis in these sentences to focus on what I see as the whole purpose for the impersonation of Jesus, and that is to deceive the waiting, praying ones. They are the only ones he has not been able to "sweep in." This move is called "Satan's last device" (1992) which indicates the lateness of the time for this last effort. I do not believe this statement can be used to substantiate the theory of his impersonation being to initiate the Sunday law. Now we will see the main reason the impersonation cannot bring in the Sunday law. The next quotation places the impersonation *after the close of probation*:

> The wrath of Satan increases as his time grows short, and his work of deceit and destruction *reaches its culmination*

> *The wrath of Satan increases as his time grows short, and his work of deceit and destruction reaches its culmination in the time of trouble. God's longsuffering has ended. The world has rejected His mercy, despised His love, and trampled upon His law. The wicked have passed the boundary of their probation, and the Lord withdraws His protection, and leaves them to the mercy of the leader they have chosen...*

in the time of trouble. God's longsuffering has ended. The world has rejected His mercy, despised His love, and trampled upon His law. The wicked have passed the boundary of their probation, and the Lord withdraws His protection, and leaves them to the mercy of the leader they have chosen...

As the crowning act in the great drama of deception, Satan himself will attempt to personate Christ. The church has long professed to look to the Savior's advent as the consummation of her hopes. Now the great deceiver will make it appear that Christ has come. (White, *The Spirit of Prophecy*, vol. 4, 1884, 441, emphasis added)

This picture of the impersonation is clear and very different from many interpretations that I have heard. Notice several important points: it is "one last desperate effort," it was at a time when "the judgement and eternity were in view" for the waiting saints because it takes place in the time of trouble. Satan *hears* "the unceasing cry for Christ to deliver them," and he employs one last effort "to make *them* think their prayers are answered." One last, all-important fact is that probation has ended, the test has been given, and the wicked have failed the test. The test is on the Commandments of God and the Sabbath in particular. The Sunday laws have already been in force. We know this because "[t]he wicked have *passed the boundary of their probation.*"

Included in this scenario is the belief that the Sunday law is passed by the influence of evil angels impersonating the dead. These angels claim that Jesus changed the Sabbath from Saturday to Sunday. There is no doubt that this deception will happen; the problem is that the focus of the manifestations is not what is commonly thought.

> The *miracle-working power manifested through spiritualism will exert its influence against those who choose to obey God rather than men*. Communications from the spirits will declare that God has sent them to convince the *rejecters of Sunday* of their error, affirming that the laws of the land should be obeyed as the law of God. They will lament the great wickedness in the world and second the testimony of religious teachers that the degraded state of morals is caused by the desecration of Sunday. Great will be the indignation excited against all who refuse to accept their testimony. (White, *Maranatha,* 1976, 167)

It is all about the people of God. It is clear the impersonation is not to establish Sunday laws; they are already in force and by now all have been tested, but instead it is to deceive the "very elect." Satan by this time owns those who have rejected God's warning. It's all over. Decisions have been made, and the time of trouble has come by the time Satan does his "crowning act."

As for the visitations from spirits, these too are aimed at the children of

> ***It is clear the impersonation is not to establish Sunday laws; they are already in force and by now all have been tested, but instead it is to deceive the "very elect."***

God, who have chosen to "obey God rather than man" and are "the rejecters of Sunday." The visits take place after they have rejected the push for Sunday exaltation. The fact that so much of Satan's work of deception happens after the close of probation including his impersonation of Christ places additional importance on the mysterious time before the close of probation—the time in which we live. Satan doesn't need to pretend to be Christ to deceive the world; he already has a masterful plan one around which the whole world is already uniting.

There was another time in history when events didn't match expectations. I'm referring to the birth and life of the Son of God. The Jews from the Pharisees to the common man on the street expected Jesus to come as conquering King and place Israel in power over the rest of the non-Jewish world. Even the disciples for the most part believed the same way. The disciples did not completely understand until after His death and resurrection.

When Christ came in the manner in which He did, the people had trouble accepting Him. Was it because they had no idea of the circumstances of His birth? Were there no prophecies about the life He would live? Actually, there were many prophecies telling of His life, and the manner of His death.

Jesus wasn't accepted by a majority of the people because they cherished a wrong understanding of what the Bible said concerning Him. They expected Him to come in the manner of His *second* coming. They were expecting Jesus to come but were mistaken about prophecies concerning *time*. But what a difference timing makes. How many were lost because of a wrong interpretation of prophecy even though they were devout students of the Bible.

Another example from history is the story of the Millerites in 1844. They were on this occasion right about time, but they were wrong about the event. God still used those from the "Great Disappointment." He used those who didn't give up but carried on until they understood their error. As we all know, our great church arose out of that misinterpretation of prophecy. So, let us be honest enough to admit that we may still have something to learn about prophecy. That we, too, could be daily expecting events to transpire based on faulty interpretation or lack of knowledge. "My people are destroyed for lack of knowledge: because thou hast rejected knowledge, I will also reject thee, that thou shalt be no priest to me: seeing thou hast forgotten the law of thy God, I will also forget thy children" (Hosea 4:6).

We have already quoted the passage from the *Great Controversy* where Satan is described as working with the elements to claim his victims. I would like to repeat some of it here in the context of justifying the environmental movement with inspired prophecy: "In accidents and calamities by sea and by land, in great conflagrations, in fierce tornadoes and terrific hailstorms, in tempests, floods, cyclones, tidal waves, and earthquakes, in every place and in a thousand forms, Satan is exercising his power. He sweeps away the ripening harvest, and famine and distress follow. *He imparts to the air a deadly taint, and thousands perish by the pestilence*" (White, *The Great Controversy,* 1911, 589).

> *Here the temperance work, one of the most prominent and important of moral reforms, is often combined with the Sunday movement*, and the advocates of the latter represent themselves as laboring to promote the highest interest of society; and those who refuse to unite with them are denounced as the enemies of temperance and reform.
>
> It is one of Satan's devices to combine with false- hood just enough truth to give it plausibility. *The leaders of the Sunday movement may advocate reforms which the people need, principles which are in harmony with the Bible*, yet while there is with these a requirement which is contrary to God's law, his servants cannot unite with them. (White, *The Great Controversy,* 1911, 587)

"*The Sunday movement is now making its way in darkness.* The leaders are concealing the true issue, and many who unite in the movement do not themselves see whither the undercurrent is tending" (White, *Counsels for the Church,* 1991, 335.2, emphasis added).

We see in these comments elements that correspond very closely to the manner in which the environmental movement is working today—steadily moving toward a Sabbath for the earth.

There is no doubt that the movement is advocating reforms we need; we should care for and preserve Gods creation. We definitely should not "relentlessly press creation" but allow it to rest as the Bible recommends. And we cannot disagree that the air has a "deadly taint," nor that thousands are dying annually from the consequences. The predictions are for many more thousands to "perish."

"Satan is working in the atmosphere; he is poisoning the atmosphere, and here we are dependent upon God for our lives—our present and eternal lives. And being in the position that we are, we need to be wide awake, wholly devoted, wholly converted, wholly consecrated to God. But we seem to sit as though we were paralyzed. God of heaven, wake us up!" (White, *Selected Messages Book 2*, 1958, 52).

> God has not restrained the powers of darkness from carrying forward their deadly work of vitiating the air, one of the sources of life and nutrition, with a deadly miasma. Not only is vegetable life affected but man suffers from pestilence....These things are the result of drops from the vials of God's wrath [God takes responsibility for that which he allows or does or does not prevent. [Exod. 7:3; 8:32; 1 Chron. 10:4, 13, 14]. being sprinkled on the earth and are but faint representations of what will be in the near future. (White, *Selected Messages Book 3*, 1980, 391)

Sometimes we read statements from the Spirit of Prophecy and tend to disregard them because the wording is not in step with modern terminology. For instance, two words from the last quotation above are words definitely from another era: "vitiate" and "miasma." Should we disregard the statements because these archaic words are used? If we choose to do so, we should discard the Scriptures as well.

When we realize what the definitions for the two words are, the statement is far more relevant today than when it was originally written. The definition for *miasma* is "*harmful fumes*: a harmful or poisonous emanation, especially one caused by *burning* or *decaying* organic matter." *Vitiate* is "to destroy or drastically reduce the effectiveness of something." Let's rewrite the statement above using modern language and notice how important they are:

"God has not restrained the powers of darkness from carrying forward their deadly work of *'reducing the effectiveness of'* the air, one of the sources of life and nutrition, with *'harmful fumes caused by burning organic matter.'*" (Known today as "fossil fuels.")

"He imparts to the air a deadly taint." "Satan is working in the atmosphere; he is poisoning the atmosphere." God told us years ago what was going to happen, and I am sure that the people in the writer's day didn't understand what she wrote any more than we seem to understand today. In the light of recent developments these statements become crystal clear. I ask the question, does the Spirit of Prophecy harmonize with the theory of an environmental Sabbath bringing in the Sunday laws? You be the judge.

We are living in the time of the end, and we know that according to prophecy events will result in Sunday laws with the U.S. leading the way. We also know that the entire world will follow our lead. The catalyst will need to be something sufficient to convince the world with all its ethnic diversity to accept the law as something we all need. If there is anything else that fits the bill more than this, I've been unable to find it.

What do the Scriptures say concerning corresponding last-day events? Is there anything to indicate an environmental connection? To begin, let's look at the most popular scriptures pertaining to the battle in the last days. It's recorded in Revelation 16:13–16.

> And I saw three unclean spirits like frogs [come] out of the mouth of the dragon, and out of the mouth of the beast, and out of the mouth of the false prophet.
>
> For they are the spirits of devils, working miracles, [which] go forth unto the kings of the earth and of the whole world, to gather them to the battle of that great day of God Almighty.
>
> Behold, I come as a thief. Blessed [is] he that watcheth, and keepeth his garments, lest he walk naked, and they see his shame.

76 | An Overwhelming Surprise

> And he gathered them together into a place called in the Hebrew tongue Armageddon.

This is the threefold alliance of evil Satan gathers against the remnant of God in the last days. There is much to be found in Scripture that shines a light on this last battle. We will return later to these three froglike creatures, but first let's look at two related events beginning with 2 Chronicles 20.

After the division of Israel, the remaining faithful were the two tribes in the south called Judah. The king, Jehoshaphat, was informed that three nations were on their way to attack. Judah would have been overwhelmed by their numbers. King Jehoshaphat called the people and led them in fasting and praying. God sent a prophetic message through Jahaziel advising him that he would not have to fight in this battle "the battle is not yours, but God's" (2 Chron. 20:15).

"Tomorrow go ye down against them: behold, they come up by the cliff of Ziz; and ye shall find them at the end of the brook, before the wilderness of Jeruel.

"Ye shall not [need] to fight in this [battle]: set yourselves, stand ye [still], and see the salvation of the LORD with you, O Judah and Jerusalem: fear not, nor be dismayed; tomorrow go out against them: for the LORD [will be] with you" (2 Chron. 20:16, 17).

In the morning, with the singers in front, the army of Judah went to the cliff before the wilderness of Jeruel as God had instructed. There they found the armies of "the children of Moab, and the children of Ammon, and with them [other] beside the Ammonites," (2 Chron. 20: 22) they were all dead. Each had killed the other.

This account is representative of the final conflict in many ways. The kingdom of Judah is the "remnant" of Israel; they were not to fight in the battle. There was a threefold enemy united to attack Judah; the only preparation needed was to humble themselves, pray, and believe; otherwise, God would do the rest.

Another account is a prophetic message found in Joel:

> Proclaim ye this among the Gentiles; Prepare war, wake up the mighty men, let all the men of war draw near; let them come up: beat your plowshares into swords, and your pruning hooks into spears: let the weak say, I [am] strong.
>
> Assemble yourselves, and come, all ye heathen, and gather yourselves together round about: thither cause thy mighty ones to come down, O LORD.
>
> Let the heathen be wakened and come up to the valley of Jehoshaphat: for there will I sit to judge all the heathen round about.
>
> Put ye in the sickle, for the harvest is ripe: come, get you down; for the press is full, the vats overflow; for their wickedness [is] great.
>
> Multitudes, multitudes in the valley of decision: for the day of the LORD [is] near in the valley of decision. (Joel 3:9–14)

This prophecy in Joel, sandwiched in Scripture between the story of Jehoshaphat and the book of Revelation's prophecy of three unclean spirits, links them both to the conditions in the last days. The prophecy in Revelation 16 presents three powers called together by the unclean spirits to battle against God's people just as it was in Jehoshaphat's day. The enemy in Joel chapter 3 is called by God to "come up" to the battle, and at the same time His "mighty ones" (His angels) are called to "come down." When you read 2 Chronicles 20, you will notice that the enemy had to also "come up" to the battle. A three-fold enemy in 2 Chronicles 20, and a threefold enemy in Revelation 16.

Now the environmental connection. In Revelation 16, the threefold enemy is called to battle by "three unclean spirits like frogs." In scripture, angels are called "ministering spirits," "unclean spirits," and "seducing spirits," with doctrines of devils. So, can we be safe to say that the "unclean spirits" of Revelation 16 are evil angels with a false doctrine? Now, why did the unclean spirits look like frogs to the prophet John? Nowhere else in Scripture are spirits compared to animals. It could have something to do with the message they bear.

In today's world the environmental movement has two symbols: the color green, and frogs. The color green is probably easy to understand, but there may be a little confusion as to why frogs. Frogs are a symbol of the environmental movement because as *Time* states in an article, "Frogs are what scientists call an indicator species: particularly sensitive animals that are the first to go when the climate starts to change. Their extinction may increase pressure on government and industry to dial back on greenhouse gases. The harlequins, after all, are only the beginning" (J. Kluger, 2006).

The subtitle of the article is "Massive Die Offs in the American Tropics are an Early Warning of the Effects of Global Warming." In other words, frogs are an environmental "early warning system."

I believe the "three unclean spirits like frogs" are carrying to "the kings of the earth and of the whole world" a message that would bring the people together in an effort to save the world from environmental disaster, and one of the measures will include a "Sabbath for the Earth." Here is something to think about first read Revelation 6:8: "And I looked, and behold a pale horse: and his name that sat on him was Death, and Hell followed with him. And power was given unto them over the fourth part of the earth, to kill with sword, and with hunger, and with death, and with the beasts of the earth." The original language from which the "pale" color is translated, is actually *green*. Much more study needs to be done concerning that bit of information.

Now let's go back to the prophecy in Joel 3. The Lord, who directs the final events, (Ezek. 1:4, 26; 10:8; Dan. 4:17, 25, 32) tells the wicked, to "beat your plowshares into swords, and your pruning hooks into spears". Plowshares and pruning hooks are clearly "garden tending" tools. Religious environmental groups refer to environmentalism as "tending the earth", and frequently refer to the earth as the "garden", and the tools are regulations for tending that "garden".

In that light, let's look at the verse they came from in Joel, transposing these meanings from the original and see what we get:

Proclaim ye this among the Gentiles; Prepare war, wake up the mighty men, let all the men of war draw near; let them come up: beat your *garden tending tools into weapons*: let the weak say, I am strong.

Assemble yourselves, and come, all ye heathen, and gather yourselves together round about: thither cause thy mighty ones to come down, O LORD.

Let the heathen be wakened and come up to the valley of Jehoshaphat: for there will I sit to judge all the heathen round about.

Put ye in the sickle, for the harvest is ripe: come, get you down; for the press is full, the vats overflow; for their wickedness is great. Multitudes, multitudes in the valley of decision: for the day of the LORD is near in the valley of decision. (Joel 3:9–14)

To say it another way, "Take the environmental measures you have been using to care for the earth and use them against the people of God."

In that day, the inhabitants of the earth will face a time of "decision." They must decide whether they will have eternal life or not. The issue that will bring them to that decision is the same issue that will determine whether they receive the mark of the beast or the seal of God.

Look again at the role of *spiritualism* in the last days. We are told that in the last days we will have to face demons appearing like the departed giving us messages from Heaven that the Sabbath was changed to Sunday. This, they say, is the roll of spiritualism.

There is no doubt that one of the threefold powers from which "three unclean spirits like frogs" shall come is represented as spiritualism. This form of spiritualism is the ungodly powers of the world in many forms with many beliefs. It is not just the act of communication with the dead.

There was a time in the early days of our denomination when pantheism was embraced by some of our leaders. In referring to the incident, the Spirit of Prophecy has this comment: "Today there are coming into educational institutions and into the churches everywhere spiritualistic teachings that undermine faith in God and in His word. The theory that God is an essence pervading all nature is received by many who profess to believe the Scriptures; but, however beautifully clothed, this theory is a most dangerous deception" (White, *The Ministry of Healing,* 1905, 428).

The theory that "God is an essence pervading all nature" is nothing more than pantheism. Many today don't realize how dangerous these teachings are. We will soon find out why. It is important to realize that the "spiritualism" aspect of the threefold enemy in Revelation can also represent the teachings which support pantheism and other pagan beliefs. To assume that it refers only to communications from the dead can block our understanding to the point that we misinterpret last-day events. The demons will play a part in the deceptions of the last days but will not be the instrument to bring about the laws. And again, the main target is the "elect."

Let's go now to the book of Revelation to a scripture typically referred to by Adventists as the "three angels' messages." We are accustomed to connecting them to a call for the observance of the Bible Sabbath as described in the Ten Commandments based on similar language found in Exodus 20. With one exception, there is no mention of the animals. There will be a call to observe the true Sabbath at the time of this angel's message. The verses I am referring to are found in Revelation 14:6, 7: "And I saw another angel fly in the midst of heaven, having the everlasting gospel to preach unto them that dwell on the earth, and to every nation, and kindred, and tongue, and people, Saying with a loud voice, Fear God, and give glory to him; for the hour of his judgment is come: and worship him that made heaven, and earth, and the sea, and the fountains of waters."

The timing of this message is just prior to the close of probation at the testing time. The call is to "worship" the "creator" God as opposed to worship of the beast. We are told to worship Him "that made heaven, and earth, and the sea, and the fountains of waters" (Rev. 14:7). It seems as though we are told to worship Him *instead* of these places. Coincidentally, these places are habitats, the environment to animals and man. These verses sound very much like the fourth commandment where man is admonished to remember the Sabbath and the God who made these things except that these verses don't mention the animals. Is it possible man will by setting up a rest day for the Earth be placing these things above the God who made them, thus, making them objects of worship? Making them gods as it were. Therefore, a call to worship the *Creator.*

We see these places mentioned again in Revelation. As with the plagues on Egypt, God sends His plagues on the things that the people are placing above Him. The things targeted in the ten plagues in Egypt were the things they worshiped typically all things of nature. As the angel says in Revelation 16:6 pertaining to the water turning to blood, "they have shed the blood of saints and prophets, and thou hast given them blood to drink." (like for like,) The beast institutes a false Sabbath and forces man to treat it as sacred while trampling on the true Sabbath. In honoring it, people were in fact worshiping the beast who is solely responsible for it. We will discuss the issue of Earth worship more in depth in a later chapter.

Referring back to a previous statement from the Spirit of Prophecy, notice that the writer refers to the work being done to the environment as drops from the wrath of God:

> God has not restrained the powers of darkness from carrying forward their deadly work of vitiating the air, one of the sources of life and nutrition, with a deadly *miasma*. Not only is vegetable life affected but man suffers from pestilence....These things are the result of *drops from the vials of God's wrath being sprinkled on the earth, and are but faint representations of what will be in the near future.* (White, *Selected Messages Book 3,* 1980, 391)

The drops from the vials of God's wrath are a representation of the plagues in the last days. "And I heard a great voice out of the temple saying to the seven angels, Go your ways, and pour out the *vials of the wrath of God* upon the earth" (Rev. 16:1).

These drops falling now, though weaker, are similar in nature to those catastrophic events at the end of time. What does this say of the "drops" falling now? In the description of the plagues, we find that the angels pour their "vials" upon "the earth," "the sea," "the rivers and fountains of water," "the sun" (scorching the earth with heat), and the "air." These are the elements of the environment which people today are striving to save by their call for a "Sabbath for the Earth." The seven last plagues are directed at the *environment*.

The last seven plagues also include one in which the wrath was poured out on the "seat of the beast." The "seat of the beast" receives a plague because the people worship it, and the beast receives this worship through the false Sabbath he established.

There is another statement from the Spirit of Prophecy that we must look at which sounds so much like today's news headlines. "In the last scenes of this earth's history, war will rage. There will be pestilence, plague, and famine. *The waters of the deep will overflow their boundaries*. Property and life will be destroyed by fire and flood" (White 1976, 174).

More and more the news pertaining to the environment is centered on the melting of polar ice and alpine glaciers, with a corresponding rise in ocean levels. Predictions of melting that raise sea levels by only three feet could "swamp low lying Pacific islands such as Tuvalu, flood large areas of Bangladesh or Florida and threaten cities from New York to Buenos Aires" (Rahmstorf, qtd. in Doyle, 2006).

Other news that places more urgency on this type of report is the fact that as new studies are revealed the rate of melting appears to be accelerating. This raises the probability that consequences of global warming (including sea-level rise) may be felt in the near or immediate future. This places more pressure on reluctant governments to pass measures to halt the process.

Here we have a prophecy of present-day phenomena resulted from global warming included in descriptions of closing events. Combined with the other statements in this chapter, this places our day at the end of time and paints a picture of a time when environmentalism impacts events sufficiently to be addressed through prophecy. All these, i.e., "deadly taint," "miasma" (or fumes from burning organic matter), calls to worship the God who created the environment, and a call to save the Earth by creating "a Sabbath for the Earth" combined construct a picture we cannot ignore.

In these last days Satan is attacking on many often very different fronts. Throughout the world, he has agents working with only one object in mind to disrupt God's plan for this world and cause His people to be lost.

> Satan's enmity against Christ has been manifested against his followers. The same hatred of the principles of God's law, the same policy of deception, *by which error is made to appear as truth, by which human laws are substituted for the law of God, and men are led to worship the creature rather than the Creator...In the great final conflict, Satan will employ the same policy, manifest the same spirit, and work for the same end,* as in all preceding ages. That which has been, will be, except that the coming struggle will be marked with a terrible intensity such as the world has never witnessed. Satan's deceptions will be more subtle, his assaults more determined. *If it were possible, he would lead astray the elect.* (White, *The Great Controversy,* 1888, introduction, emphasis added)

Notice how Satan worked in the past: "human laws are substituted for the law of God, and men are led to worship the creature rather than the Creator," and "in the great final conflict, Satan will employ the same policy, manifest the same spirit, and work for the same end" as he has in times past.

At this time Satan is consolidating his forces bringing as many as he can under one umbrella. Each individual element of this effort is able to retain its individuality or diversity—as the environmentalists call it today. The impression given is that suddenly all these diverse organizations have spontaneously converged to work for the "common good" when in reality they have been *called together* for the last great battle against the people of God as seen by the prophets Joel and John.

Although we are focusing on the issue of global warming in this work, we will be looking into various other issues that are being carried along with the environmental movement. Some of these issues are no less serious than the "Sabbath for the Earth" issue. The following quotation gives us a clue as to what some of those issues may be:

> *The experience of the* past will be repeated. In the future, Satan's superstitions will assume new forms. Errors will be presented in a pleasing and flattering manner. False theories, clothed with garments of light, will be presented to God's people. Thus Satan will try to deceive, if possible, the very elect. Most seducing influences will be exerted; minds will be hypnotized.
>
> *The exaltation of nature as God, the unrestrained license of the human will, the counsel of the ungodly*— these Satan uses as agencies to bring about certain ends. He will employ the power of mind over mind to carry out his designs. The most sorrowful thought of all is that under his deceptive influence <u>men will have a form of godliness, without having a real connection with God</u>. Like Adam and Eve, who ate the fruit from the tree of the knowledge of good and evil, many are even now feeding upon the deceptive morsels of error. (White, *The Review and Herald,* March 3, 1904, para. 1, 2, emphasis added)

If we study events of the past to see how Satan has deceived people, we can have insight into how he will attempt to deceive us. He will use some of the same devices he used before. There is nothing new under the sun.

In his description of what man would be like at the end of time, Paul says that men would have "a form of godliness but denying the power thereof" (2 Tim. 3:5).

Slowly, the human race is uniting the religions of the world into this type of religion and erasing all the distinguishing characteristics of doctrine which leaves a bland, lifeless form of religion. All this is done under the guise of the "common good." Strange things can happen when man denies the only true God.

We understand that God has people scattered among all the churches in the world. They are faced with the decision of whom they will obey—God and His laws or man and the laws of man inspired by the "man of sin" (2 Thess. 2:3). For any who see these things taking place, my message is to read the Scriptures and be sure on which side you are standing.

The Bible tells of a time when man will experience a "time of trouble" like none before, throughout the entire history of the world. All who live at that time will experience the "trouble," but those who receive the mark of the beast will have the most to suffer, namely, the separation from the Father that broke the heart of Jesus as He hung upon the cross. Please, study things out for yourself.

CHAPTER 7

Golden Opportunity or Missed Opportunity

The environmental crisis with a demand for answers is racing toward us like a giant tsunami. Moving at the speed of a jet airliner, a tsunami is nearly unrecognizable with only a slight rise in the ocean surface. This continues until the wave nears land at which time its dangerous hidden character is revealed.

Upon reaching shore, the first thing to notice is a receding shoreline. The receding shoreline draws many out to investigate like a predator dangling bait in the face of its intended victim. Suddenly the water returns and with it the wave. Having traveled sometimes hundreds of miles nearly imperceptibly, the wave now rushes on shore like a giant roaring river sometimes several stories high carrying with it everything in its path.

What was once a gentle swell quietly speeding across the ocean's clear waters has now become a gigantic, deadly flow across the land. It is a flow full of sand, trees, houses, motor vehicles—a deadly composite of everything on the earth's surface.

This is how the environmental movement has been moving through the pages of recent history. At first a very low hardly noticeable profile, but, recently, it has been rising up gaining the spotlight and attention of all the inhabitants of this troubled world. It is on the verge of overwhelmingly rushing upon us thrusting upon us its cargo of deception, fear, and anti-Christian philosophy.

What has been perceived as a movement simply for the care of our environment has upon closer investigation been found to contain elements of paganism, spiritualism, and secularism which threaten to change our world irreversibly. When this crisis rushes upon the world in its fully matured form, we as the remnant followers of our creator God will have an opportunity and an obligation to enlighten the world as to the true worship of the Creator. This opportunity will be unlike any we have ever had.

The issues to be confronted will open doors that have been closed for centuries. When a call for laws requiring a rest day for the Earth become a part of the legislative process, the light on the true Sabbath will shine everywhere. When this does happen, we will need to be prepared. We will need to understand the issues involved. "Study to show thyself approved" says the Scriptures (2 Tim. 2:15). When needed, the Holy Spirit will bring to mind all that has been previously committed to memory.

What has been perceived as a movement simply for the care of our environment has upon closer investigation been found to contain elements of paganism, spiritualism, and secularism which threaten to change our world irreversibly.

One of the biggest questions to arise from the environmental crisis is, who is to blame? This question provides a perfect opportunity to discuss the condition of the world today—much like the world before the flood—corrupted and rampaged by sin. This "crisis" provides a platform for exposing the ills of a world gone astray, but where are those crying out?

Many environmental leaders say the Christian church is to blame. Prominent leaders such as Lynn White, Jr. and Thomas Berry are quick to point out what they say is a weakness in Christianity which makes us an enemy of the environment. Lynn White, Jr. says,

> I personally doubt that disastrous ecologic backlash can be avoided simply by applying to our problems more science

and more technology. Our science and technology have grown out of Christian attitudes toward man's relation to nature...

However, the present increasing disruption of the global environment is the product of a dynamic technology and science which were originating in the Western medieval world...Their growth cannot be understood historically apart from distinctive attitudes toward nature which are deeply grounded in Christian dogma. The fact that most people do not think of these attitudes as Christian is irrelevant. No new set of basic values has been accepted in our society to displace those of Christianity. Hence, we shall continue to have a worsening ecologic crisis until we reject the Christian axiom that nature has no reason for existence save to serve man. (1967, 1203–1207)

> *Many concerned people, convinced that environmental problems are more spiritual than technological, are exploring the world's ideologies and religions in search of non-Christian spiritual resources for the healing of the earth.*

How interesting! The root of the ecological crisis comes from Christianity. The worst thing about this idea is that many of the Christian leaders in this country accept this theory. They apologize and begin to seek ways to alter the Christian view of the Creation. A statement from the *Evangelical Environmental Network & Creation Care Magazine* says, "Many concerned people, convinced that environmental problems are more spiritual than technological, are exploring the world's ideologies and religions in search of non-Christian spiritual resources for the healing of the earth" (Gottlieb, *This Sacred Earth,* 224).

Well, what could we expect? If the ecological problem is caused by the Christian world, then, surely we should look to other areas for solutions. Some even go to the extreme of advocating that "[r]eligions, thus need to be reexamined in light of the current environmental crisis" (Tucker and Grim, 1997). Not only are we accused of creating the problem, but now we are advised to seek help from "non-Christian spiritual resources," and we need to be "reexamined" with the environmental crisis as an incentive. They say it is because we worship a God who is above and beyond the earth. We expect this same God to redeem us from this earth at some future time, and that we must be the problem. I don't deny the fact that some who call themselves Christians have no difficulty destroying God's wonderful world. They don't do so because they are "Christians," but they do so because they really aren't Christian even though they claim to be.

By accepting blame for the crisis and endeavoring to correct the problem from within the church, the Christian churches are missing a golden opportunity. We are passing up a chance to enlighten the world as to what truly is wrong. The problem is not Christian, Jew, Muslim, or Buddhist but man and sin.

When God created the world, He provided for man an owner's manual which if read and followed would have kept this world in perfect operating condition. Even with the entrance of sin, if the plan had been known and followed to the best of the ability of sinful man this would still be a different world.

When the nation of Israel was in its heyday there was nothing like it on the face of the earth. This was at the time of King Solomon when Israel was what God had intended it should be—a light to the nations round about. This was typified by the visit of the Queen of Sheba to see if what she had heard was true. What she saw was much more than she had expected, and inspired from her we have this statement from 1 Kings 10:6,7,9: "And she said to the king, It was a true report that I heard in mine own land of thy acts and of thy wisdom. Howbeit I believed not the words, until I came, and mine eyes had seen [it]: and, behold, the half was not told me: thy wisdom and prosperity exceedeth the fame which I heard. Blessed be the LORD thy God, which delighted in thee, to set thee on the throne of Israel: because the LORD loved Israel forever, therefore made he thee king, to do judgment and justice."

How wonderful things would be if we could just obey the Lord our Creator. But how dysfunctional it is without His blessing and approval. This world has been in rebellion against God and His law since the fall of our first parents. Not only has there been sin from the erring race but also open rebellion with an overwhelming dislike for our God, His laws, and everything He does or says.

Sinful man in reckless abandon has raced headlong into a life completely devoid of knowing or desiring to do the will of God. He has done all within his ability to erase even the slightest reminder of the Creator. He has instead gathered to himself all that would offer or suggest another reality. This he does in every aspect of life. Beginning with the innocent child and moving from kindergarten through the highest levels of education, man has arranged things in such a way that as much as possible he isn't reminded of God and His requirements. Paul describes the process well in 2 Timothy 4:3, 4: "For the time will come when they will not endure sound doctrine; but after their own lusts shall they heap to themselves teachers, having itching ears; And they shall turn away their ears from the truth, and shall be turned unto fables."

This is the world in which we live. Fables are the new truth while Biblical knowledge and wisdom are now considered fables. Even in theological circles, the Scriptures, if not entirely discarded, are placed on a level below the wisdom of man.

The natural heart when unrestrained has only one god—self. Now, as in the days of Noah, the thoughts of man are only "evil continually" (Gen. 6:5). Those thoughts are centered on what will satisfy his greed or ambition and what things that will increase his wealth or comfort, and without the restraining influence of a merciful, loving God, his efforts are without concern for how others are affected. Thus, the sweat shops (industries pouring poisons into air, water and into the bodies of workers) —all in the name of profits and a few more dollars in a bank account—already have large enough to provide a comfortable living for hundreds of their workers' families.

Greed destroys the land and scours the ocean floor wiping out fish populations; manufactures and drives of giant gas guzzlers threaten to flood the homes of millions in undeveloped countries.

Greed strips clear mountain tops in an already poor area of this nation poisoning the water of nearby neighbors and destroying streams and habitats for animals in the wild. Pride builds homes that would rival some hotels in size and energy consumption which house one family of maybe four persons. This requires more lumber and resources torn from the Earth and forest already pressed to the limit. Desire for wealth, a worldly lifestyle, or a climb up the social ladder crowd many into metropolitan centers along with those who know no other home.

The cities of the world are centers of crime, pollution, and immorality pumping out waste in such quantities that systems for handling it are overwhelmed. the overflow ends up in the oceans resulting in disease and destruction of habitat. Environmentalists are concerned and, rightly so, about unhealthy industrial farms where hundreds of thousands of animals are raised in small, crowded spaces. These produce unimaginable amounts of waste that at some time or other ends up in neighboring waterways which kill thousands of fish and upset the ecological balance of the local environment. Are not the large cities of the world of much the same nature?

The greatest environmental program would be a program that changes the hearts of men. If a man claims to be a Christian and by his lifestyle is destructive to the environment, the problem is that despite his claim he is not a Christian. He is acting on his sinful human nature. Sin began the decline in the Garden of Eden, and ever since, the world has been in a state of deterioration.

Modern science teaches us that this world began in a state of confusion and is gradually getting better, but this doesn't correspond to the Second law of Thermodynamics which states that all systems will tend toward the most mathematically probable state, and eventually become totally random and disorganized.

The world is gradually deteriorating and "waxing old" like a garment (White, *Testimonies for the Church, vol. 6*, 1901). The actions of man are amplifying that rate of decline. A world in rebellion charting a course away from the divine destination, cannot and will not realize the final goal God has set. So, as modern civilization tries to place the blame for the mess we are in on the back of Christians, the actual reason is the wayward path they have chosen themselves. "Whatever a man sows," the Bible says, "that shall he also reap" (Gal. 6:7).

There is no doubt that we as Christians should be the leaders in environmental efforts if for no other reason than to care and protect those less fortunate and more vulnerable. When God gave man "dominion" over the earth, He never intended for him to misapply his commission. There have been some like those who misinterpret the scriptures about the authority of husbands over their wives who also misinterpret the scripture concerning "dominion." This is likely the only realistic grounds opponents of Christianity have for naming us as the cause of the crisis.

We as repositories of God's Word and Spirit need to be using this opportunity to reach those who may be open to receiving the word and are concerned with the direction this world appears to be headed. We must trust in the knowledge God has given us and the way man should be living in light of current events. Those of "non-Christian spiritual" sources have no more at their disposal than we.

What an opportune time to give the messages, such as: "For what is a man profited, if he shall gain the whole world, and lose his own soul?" Or, "What shall a man give in exchange for his soul?" (Mark 8:36). Or, "There is a way that seemeth right unto a man, but the end thereof is the way of death" (Prov. 4:12). Man must be reached with the message that Jesus is coming soon, and that those who disregard His laws and teach men to do the same will feel the wrath of God. People must be warned that what God required of the human race in years past in reference to the commandments is still required today. The word of God has a lot to offer a troubled world—a world with far more problems than the environment alone.

When God decided to destroy the earth in the days of Noah, He didn't tell Noah to choose the driest, windiest day of the year to select a choice group, give each a torch, and set fire to the earth and wicked. Instead, Noah was to make a way of escape for the people. The remnant church is to do the job Noah was instructed to do. The remnant church is an ark of safety in this time when

God will soon be coming to "destroy those who destroy the earth" (Rev. 11:18).

As public apprehension rises over the possibility of drastic changes to our planet home, we must warn them of the major changes that are coming with the final crisis culminating with the second coming of our glorious Redeemer. These are changes that will include a test to determine who will receive the seal of God or the mark of the beast. Revelation illustrates how serious will be the time when consequences come to those who have the mark. This is the real crisis the world is facing. Rather than waste our time trying to appease those who are determined that Christians are responsible for the crisis, we need to be warning the rejectors of God's law and His authority. These times require a straight testimony. According to the Spirit of Prophecy, "God does not send messengers to flatter the sinner. He delivers no message of peace to lull the unsanctified into fatal security" (White, *The Desire of Ages,* 1898, 104). We have a church to prepare and a world to warn.

> For the wrath of God is revealed from heaven against all ungodliness and unrighteousness of men, who hold the truth in unrighteousness;
>
> Because that which may be known of God is manifest in them; for God hath showed it unto them.
>
> For the invisible things of him from the creation of the world are clearly seen, being understood by the things that are made, even his eternal power and God- head; so that they are without excuse:
>
> Because that, when they knew God, they glorified him not as God, neither were thankful; but became vain in their imaginations, and their foolish heart was darkened. Professing themselves to be wise, they became fools. (Rom. 1:18–22)

We must understand what the doctrines of the church are in relation to the issues and be prepared to give the world one last warning.

We must all have our eyes wide open in the area of environmentalism. We should enter into no programs or sign on to any statements which we haven't thoroughly studied in the context of our Biblical foundation. Under the surface are programs and ideologies which are very unbiblical to say the least.

We need to be wide awake. As the Lord's messenger said when revealing Satan's work with the atmosphere, "Satan is working in the atmosphere; he is poisoning the atmosphere, and here we are dependent upon God for our lives—our present and eternal lives. And being in the position that we are, *we need to be wide awake, wholly devoted, wholly converted, wholly consecrated to God*. But we seem to sit as though we were paralyzed. God of heaven, *wake us up*" (White, *Selected Messages Book 2,* 1958, 52, emphasis added).

Many will not awaken until it is too late. We go from day to day like the antediluvians with our focus on the things of this life. This warning of the Apostle Luke is applicable to us today: "And take heed to yourselves, lest at any time your hearts be overcharged with surfeiting, and drunkenness, and cares of this life, and so that day come upon you unawares. For as a snare shall it come on all them that dwell on the face of the whole earth. Watch ye therefore, and pray always, that ye may be accounted worthy to escape all these things that shall come to pass, and to stand before the Son of man" (Luke 21:34–36).

Watch and pray, Luke says; why? Because it *will* come like a snare upon "all them that dwell on the face of the whole earth," and not just the ungodly, it includes us. A snare is a trap built into the surroundings (or environment) in such a way as to make it invisible. The prey has no idea the trap is there until it is too late. Going about its every day life, the victim has no idea of the danger it is in. So, it is with us!

The world races headlong toward destruction, and we are so wrapped up in the "cares of this life" that we, first, don't see the danger, and, second, live so much like the world that we see things in "nearly the same light."

Some day we will be calling God's people out of Babylon. How can we do that if we don't have anything better to offer? The environmental crisis and the coming "Sabbath for the Earth" is the proverbial "golden opportunity" for the people of God to reach the world on the issue of the true Creator God. We should be prepared to spread the word about the true Sabbath of the Decalogue—the Sabbath of creation week. We have worked under sometimes very stiff opposition to reach and teach people about the true Sabbath, how it was changed by the Papal power, and how it will be a test to determine who will receive the seal of God.

When the issue of enforcing a Sabbath for the earth is introduced, the door will be wide open to spread the news of the Sabbath. The only problem is that we may not be ready. It is also possible; we may not recognize the opportunity because we are not alert to what is happening. The inspired author speaking of the circulation of the book *The Great Controversy* makes this statement:

> By reading it, some souls will be aroused, and will have courage to unite themselves at once with those who keep the commandments of God. But a much larger number who read it will not take their position until *they see the very events taking place that are foretold* in it. The fulfillment of some of the predictions will inspire faith that others also will come to pass, and when the earth is lightened with the glory of the Lord, in the closing work, many souls will take their position on the commandments of God as the result of this agency. (White, *Last Day Events,* 1992, 214)

It is my prayer that the material presented in this book will be the very first fulfillment of this prophecy.

Trying times and great opportunities are just before us. The wicked are not the only people to be warned. This crisis is a perfect opportunity to warn those in the church who in their lives have, as Israel in the time of Elijah, forgotten the God of creation and accepted the beliefs of the world around them. The message to them is the same that Elijah presented to the Israelites. "And Elijah came unto all the people, and said, how long halt ye between two opinions? if the LORD [be] God, follow him: but if Baal, [then] follow him. And the people answered him not a word" (1 Kings 18:21).

The people of God now in this time of environmental crisis like Israel at the time of Elijah—and the three-year drought—must make a decision whether we will follow the word of the Lord or the influence of the world. So long have we lived in the world, worked with it, enjoyed its amusements, participated of its spirit, and more, but now if all indicators are correct, we will need to face the prospect of leaving this world. In that case, we will have to take a long careful look at ourselves to see where we stand. What will it take to get us ready? This is what we need to preach from our pulpits and from our literature. This is no time to be preaching "feelgood" sermons! That time in church every week needs to be spent addressing issues of eternal proportions.

To the leadership of the church I have this advice:

> Now is not the time to allow ourselves to be bound together with other religious organizations.
>
> Great blindness is upon the churches, and the Lord says to His people, "What agreement hath the temple of God with idols? for ye are the temple of the living God; as God hath said, I will dwell in them, and walk in them; and I will be their God, and they shall be My people. Wherefore come out from among them, and be ye separate, saith the Lord, and touch not the unclean thing; and I will receive you, and will be a father unto you, and ye shall be My sons and daughters, saith the Lord Almighty.
>
> The condition of being received into the Lord's family is coming out from the world, separating from all its contaminating influences. *The people of God are to have no connection with idolatry in any of its forms. They are to reach a higher standard. We are to be distinguished from the world, and then God says, 'I will receive you as members of My royal family, children of the heavenly King.'* As believers in the truth we are to be distinct in practice from sin and sinners. Our citizenship is in heaven. (White, *Fundamentals of Christian Education,* 1923, 481)

"Let God's people take heed that they do not sign a truce with the enemy of God and man. *The church is not to come down to take a position with the world in its ideas, opinions, and maxims.* Hear the words of Christ through his servant Paul: 'Be ye not unequally yoked together with unbelievers'...While this scripture has special reference to marriage with unbelievers, it also covers all grounds of alliance with the world" (White, *The Review and Herald,* July 31, 1894).

When Jesus came to this earth to save the people, He in no way formed any "alliances" with the religious leaders of the day. Surely, He could have done things differently forming partnerships with them, treating them as equals, and denying their backsliding. But, Jesus did nothing that would improve His standing in the world.

I understand the need to feel accepted by our contemporaries and a desire to have influence for good among them, but to form an alliance with someone implies agreement. "Can two walk together, except they be agreed?" (Amos 3:3). How can we be in agreement with those who teach that the commandments of God are no longer binding and declare the sacredness of a false Sabbath in place of the Sabbath God sanctified. If we are in an alliance with them, are we not implying that they are okay?

We have a message of warning to give the world. How can this be done if we are "unequally yoked" together with them? We need to be in a position to unreservedly give the warning about worshiping the beast and receiving his mark. When we form an alliance with other churches for the purpose of caring for the environment and we ask the government to do something to correct global warming, what position does that put us in when they institute a "sabbath for the Earth"? Haven't we asked the government to correct the problem?

We don't have to be like the world to fulfill our commission. All we need is to be like the Redeemer. If we have Jesus as our pattern, it makes no difference what the world thinks about us. When Jesus was living among men, the majority of the religious world hated Him. If we are like the world, they will like us because the world loves its own. Jesus says: "[B]ut I have chosen you out of the world, therefore the world hateth you." "Yea, and all that will live godly in Christ Jesus shall suffer persecution" (John 51:19, 2 Tim. 3:12).

> The wicked are being bound up in bundles, up in trusts, in unions, in confederacies. Let us have nothing to do with these organizations. God is our Ruler, our Governor, and He calls us to come out from the world and be separate. "Come out from among them, and be ye separate, saith the Lord, and touch not the unclean thing." If we refuse to do this, if we continue to link up with the world, and to look at every matter from a worldly standpoint, we shall become like the world. When worldly policy and worldly ideas govern our transactions, we cannot stand on the high and holy platform of eternal truth. (White, *Counsels from the Spirit of Prophecy on Labor Unions and Confederacies,* 1969)

Do we "reflect the image of Jesus fully"? This should be our concern. Let's not make the mistake of allowing ourselves to be bound with others into the "bundles" being prepared for the fires in the last day when the wheat is separated from the tares (Matt. 13:24–30). As I mentioned earlier, this environmental movement involves more danger than a sabbath for the earth. Our enemy is very sly. His purpose is to deceive the very elect. He will use every trick he has ever imagined to accomplish that goal. Let us not underestimate his talents.

It is my prayer that those, who read this book and are impressed that we are seeing the first movement toward a national Sunday law, will be inspired to take action appropriate for the time in which we are living. I hope they work to redeem the time and let their actions reveal that they are preparing for the last crisis. How could we carry on with business as usual with the prospects right before us of the very last conflict in the drama of the ages—a conflict in which we will be the primary players? Wow, what a prospect!

Voices are needed to prepare a people who will be ready to speak out. We need knowledgeable people ready with answers as circumstances warrant and ready to give the three angels' messages calling people back to worshiping the creator God. Now is the time of preparation. We must not let that time come upon us unawares. We must be ready to take advantage of this great, golden opportunity.

CHAPTER 8

More Hidden Dangers

The prince of this world is preparing his forces; he is an accomplished commander. He has a war plan honed by years of conflict with the Commander of Heaven and Earth. He has battled the children of the King since the first pair were expelled from the Garden of Eden. In addition, he has studied human nature and knows our every weakness

Like any well-prepared enemy, he is not focusing all his efforts into one issue. But many times, the separate prongs of his attack are related. That is the case with the environmental crisis. The inspiration of the Spirit of Prophecy over a hundred years ago was shown a glimpse of how Satan would work in these times.

> The experience of the past will be repeated. In the future, Satan's superstitions will assume new forms. Errors will be presented in a pleasing and flattering manner. False theories, clothed with garments of light, will be presented to God's people. Thus Satan will try to deceive, if possible, the very elect. Most seducing influences will be exerted; minds will be hypnotized.
>
> Corruptions of every type, similar to those existing among the antediluvians, will be brought in to take minds captive. The exaltation of nature as God, the unrestrained license of the human will, the counsel of the ungodly—these Satan uses as agencies to bring about certain ends. He will employ the power of mind over mind to carry out his designs. The most sorrowful thought of all is that under his deceptive influence men will have a form of godliness, without having

a real connection with God. Like Adam and Eve, who ate the fruit from the tree of the knowledge of good and evil, many are even now feeding upon the deceptive morsels of error. (White, *Testimonies for the Church, vol. 8,* 1904, 293)

The issue appears relatively clear, but a closer look will reveal other aspects of the movement which involve different issues of just as grave a nature as a Sabbath for the Earth. Stealthily Satan is using the environmental issues to lead the people of the world back to practices which were instrumental in bringing down the wrath of God upon the antediluvian world.

Separated from God and denied face to face communion—as Adam and Eve had— the rebellious human race began to deny the existence of a creator God. Left to their perverted imaginations they soon began to choose their own gods. Thus, began man's long fascination with nature worship.

From its early days, environmentalism has been hand in hand with pagan forms of earth worship. The first environmentalists were closely linked with witchcraft because of its close ties with the earth and according to *Encyclopedia Encarta:* "Many followers of the ecological and feminist movements found in Wicca a religion with congenial themes...Wiccans emphasized the sacred meanings of nature and its cycles...Wicca perceives itself a religion based on the broad themes of ancient pre-Christian paganism."

According to the *Merriam-Webster Dictionary,* paganism is believing in or relating to an ancient polytheistic or pantheistic religion. Creeping into their dialogue through environmentalism, atheists and Christian churches are embracing pagan theories. Repeating a statement quoted in the *Evangelical Environmental Network & Creation Care Magazine,* "Many concerned people, convinced that environmental problems are more spiritual than technological, are exploring the world's ideologies and religions in search of non-Christian spiritual resources for the healing of the earth." Not only are they searching, but they have found and adopted some of this philosophy.

To describe how thoroughly the pagan influence has infiltrated the churches of this country, I would like to bring you a few eye-

More Hidden Dangers | 101

opening comments from a letter circulated by the National Council of Churches. The letter begins with an assessment of the situation:

> God's creation delivers unsettling news. Earth's climate is warming to dangerous levels; 90 percent of the world's fisheries have been depleted; coastal development and pollution are causing a sharp decline in ocean health; shrinking habitat threatens to extinguish thousands of species; over 95 percent of the contiguous United States forests have been lost; and almost half of the population in the United States lives in areas that do not meet national air quality standards. In recent years the profound danger has grown, requiring us as theologians, pastors, and religious leaders to speak out and act with new urgency...We firmly believe that addressing the degradation of God's sacred earth is *the* moral assignment of our time comparable to the Civil Rights struggles of the 1960s, the worldwide movement to achieve equality for women, or ongoing efforts to control weapons of mass destruction in a post-Hiroshima world. (2005)

We firmly believe that addressing the degradation of God's sacred earth is the moral assignment of our time comparable to the Civil Rights struggles of the 1960s.

Then, the letter goes on to recommend solutions, "We believe the created world is sacred—a revelation of God's power and gracious presence filling all things [that's pantheism]. This sacred quality of creation demands moderation [also known as temperance] and sharing, urgent antidotes for our excess in consumption and waste, reminding us that economic justice is an essential condition of ecological integrity" (2005).

Under a subheading titled "Frugality," we get this advice: "Frugality connotes moderation, sufficiency, and temperance"

(2005) There is the temperance word again. Remember that the "temperance work is often combined with the Sunday movement" (White, *The Great Controversy,* 1888) as previously stated from the *Spirit of Prophecy.*

Later on we get these statements: "In this most critical moment in Earth's history, we are convinced that *the central moral imperative* of our time is the care for Earth as God's creation... We are called to worship God with all our being and actions, and to treat creation as sacred...We believe that caring for creation must undergird, and be entwined with, all other dimensions of our churches' ministries" (National Council of Churches, 2005). Then, the letter closes by the author calling for a restoring of the Earth "the greatest healing work and moral assignment of our time" (2005).

> *In this most critical moment in Earth's history, we are convinced that the central moral imperative of our time is the care for Earth as God's creation...We are called to worship God with all our being and actions, and to treat creation as sacred...*

The letter was signed by 16 prominent ministers and professors of theology from a wide range of denominations in the U.S. and Canada

Did you catch the pantheistic leaning in many of the statements? "God's power and gracious presence filling all things." There could be no clearer statement of pantheism. Despite the major moral decline in the world today, the NCC sees the environment as the most important of moral issues facing the church today.

In an article by Diane E. Sherwood, she quotes theologian Nelson Reppert and Matthew Fox, O.P., as saying that "Jesus' incarnation is the archetype of the divine presence and agency dwelling in the midst of all reality" and "the environment is a divine womb, holy and worthy of reverence and respect" (May 13, 1987).

Dieter T. Hessel from the Forum on Religion and Ecology at Harvard Divinity School makes this statement: "Ecojustice, the focus of several recent publications, offers a dynamic framework for thought and action that fosters ecological integrity with socioeconomic justice through constructive human responses serving both environmental health and social equity...Such Christian praxis discards religious beliefs and rituals that are solely preoccupied with human salvation and challenges expressions of grassroots environmentalism or of religious community that are indifferent to socioeconomic justice...for the good of the commons."

Wow! "Discards religious beliefs and rituals that are solely preoccupied with human salvation." Isn't that what Christianity is all about? Jesus came and died for "human salvation." I don't remember anything in Scripture about Jesus dying for the Earth.

God cursed the Earth for man's sake (Gen. 3:17). God does care for the earth, but the Earth is not more important to Him than the salvation of the human race. In fact, Revelation tells us of a time when the earth would pass away (Rev. 21:1). Peter says, "Heavens shall pass away with a great noise, and the elements shall melt with fervent heat, the earth also and the works that are therein shall be burned up" (2 Peter 3:10).

Why do you think people who have the Scriptures, the plain statements concerning the relation of God to the human race, and the final end of the earth and its re-creation would make such compromising statements? The answer may be found in a statement from another article in the *Forum on Religion and Ecology* by J. Baird Callicott of the University of Texas. The author is discussing comments by Lynn White, Jr. when this comment is made: "White believed that one had to identify and criticize the inherited attitudes and values regarding the characteristics of nature, human nature, and the relationship between humanity and nature that underlie and subtly shape our behavior toward the natural world. To do this, one must recognize, that the *Bible is only one of many Western sources* expounding such values, and it is perhaps *less important* than other historical sources such as Greek philosophy, the Enlightenment, modern science, capitalism, consumerism, and patriarchy" 2000, emphasis added).

Well, it's easy to see why Biblical statements have little impact on some in positions of spiritual leadership. In these comments, we see that creation is highly elevated by many involved in the environmental movement today, even those from the religious community, while the Holy Bible is placed on a level lower than secular books of history.

This is one of the hidden dangers accompanying the environ mental movement. It appears that all religious or philosophical viewpoints are welcome in the discussion except those of fundamental Christianity and the scriptures. The role of the Bible and biblically inspired writings is greatly downplayed. The day is fast approaching when an argument that a belief is supported or condemned by the Bible will no longer be grounds for consideration even among theologians. If many of the theories and philosophies encouraged by the environmental movement are to be used as arguments for the establishment of laws, the Bible undoubtedly will need to be, at the least, ignored.

The creation cannot be elevated to the level of "sacred" based on Scripture. Neither can a law establish a Sabbath for the Earth. In times past, God allowed a Sabbath year to give the land rest, but a weekly Sabbath was, as Scripture says, "made for man" (Mark 2:27).

According to the Web of Creation—an ecological website for various churches—there is a team of scholars in Adelaide, South Australia, who are developing the "Earth Bible." Their article states, "In this significant new series, writers from around the world read the Bible from the perspective of justice for Earth. Ecojustice principles are used as guidelines as they ask questions of the text: Does a given text value or de-value Earth? Is the voice of Earth heard or sup- pressed? Are humans portrayed as 'rulers' over Earth or kin with Earth? Does Earth suffer unjustly?"

How interesting that the earth has suddenly become the central focus of the Bible. The article continues by expressing the aims of the Earth Bible project. The article goes on to describe the process which "explores text and tradition from the perspectives of the Earth, employing a set of ecojustice principles developed in consultation with ecologists, *suspecting that the text and/or its interpreters may be anthropocentric and not geocentric* [In other words, what is the focus, humans or the earth?], but searching to retrieve alternate *traditions that hear the voice of Earth* and value Earth as more than a human instrument" (emphasis added).

Isn't it shocking that scholars are consulting with ecologists in order to interpret the Bible? Keep in mind what the article above says while you read the next statements from another religious source. This information comes from a roundtable report from Earth Charter Dialogues Forum. According to the report "[t]he Earth Dialogues is a public forum initiated by Mikhail Gorbachev and Maurice Strong which aims to provoke a global mobilization to further the achievements of three objectives essential to the future of humanity: averting the ecological disasters which threaten our planet; fighting the plague of poverty; and acting to ensure truly sustainable development" (2002).

The summary of the roundtable accused religion of being part of the ecological problem and was more than willing to offer some solutions which I am sure you will find interesting. Here are a few:

"Clearly our worldviews and ethics of intolerant righteousness and of greed and short term gain cannot lead us to sustainable development, despite enduring beliefs in the one right religion or the invisible hand."

"Roundtable participants agreed that institutionalized religions have many internal challenges to face." Then several "challenges" were listed:

"Fundamentalism and misdirected zealotry complicate the world scene.

"In their fundamentalist-fanatical forms, religions throughout history have justified terrorism, in jihads and crusades against people who hold different beliefs and against the earth itself" (2002).

Under the subheading "Contribution of Religions and Spiritual Groups,"

[S]urely the religious communities can also become significant partners in identifying a compelling ethical vision for sustainable life on the planet. This is their challenge and ours. For they are called now to help us move *from an exclusive preoccupation with Divine human relations and even human-human relations to renewed human-earth relations.* From a concern for a human ethic regarding homicide, suicide and genocide we are turning to a global ethics addressing biocide and geocide. This requires the voices of the spiritual traditions along with secular humanism. *This extension of ethics outward represents a major transformation for the worlds religions...* And the earth charter embodies this great transformation...As the Earth Charter suggests in the Preamble, 'Humanity is part of a vast evolving universe'...the human heart is waiting to participate in dialogue with the earth. The human soul is poised to recover the language of the sacred...And thus as the world's religions suggest our response to the earth is one of continued *gratitude for the gift of life.* (2002, emphasis added)

We will see more about the Earth Charter later in the book.

My guess is that you had no idea that the world's religions were so concerned about having "dialogue with the earth," and redirecting our focus from "Divine-human relations" or "human-human relations" to purely "human-earth relations." I ask the question, what problems will be solved by taking our attention away from the Creator and refocusing it on that which He made? And how could anyone who believes in God think to offer to the Earth their "continued gratitude for the gift of life"?

John, through inspiration, recorded the three angels' messages in the book of Revelation. One of the messages calls for us to "worship him that made heaven, and earth, and the sea, and the fountains of waters" (Rev. 14:7). Much of the religious world today appears determined to lead us to direct our attention to the creation and forget about a single powerful God—a God that instructs and demands obedience.

Satan is doing his very best to erase God's image from man, and in so doing also erase God's requirements. He is trying to enlist humans in the theory that it doesn't matter what we believe or how we worship. He wants us to believe that all efforts are accepted whether we worship the Creator or the created.

There is no doubt that the world's religions are in a state of transformation. The New Age and other pagan forms of religion are exerting a tremendous influence upon the Judeo-Christian churches, and no other means has been as successful as the environmental movement. The frightening aspect of this issue is that many of the churches are being duped, and they don't even know it. Their members for the most part are unaware because they have been so accustomed to letting the church leadership, pastors and theologians, do their thinking for them. If the pastor doesn't see a problem in it, then why should they be concerned?

Notice this statement from Mary Evelyn Tucker and John Grim, Graduate Theological Union Visiting Scholars to the Forum on Religion and Ecology Harvard University:

> One of the greatest challenges to contemporary religions, then, is how to respond to the environmental crisis...the medieval historian Lynn White has suggested that the emphasis in Judaism and Christianity on the transcendence of God above nature and the dominion of humans over nature has led to a devaluing of the natural world and a subsequent destruction of its resources for utilitarian ends...it is increasingly clear that the environmental crisis presents a serious challenge to the world's religions. This is especially true because many of these religions have traditionally been concerned with the paths of personal salvation which frequently emphasize other worldly goals and reject this world as corrupting.
>
> How to adapt religious teachings to this task of revaluing nature so as to prevent its destruction marks a significant new phase in religious thought. Indeed, as the historian of religions, Thomas Berry, has so aptly pointed out, what is necessary is a comprehensive reevaluation of human-earth relations if the human is to continue as a viable species on an increasingly degraded planet. (1997)

The statement above, that condemns *fundamentalism,* is important. This term has come to represent those out of step with the rest of the world; fanatics bent on the destruction of our way of life. This is the category the world will soon be placing us in.

There was a time when most of the protestant churches could be called fundamentalist. Things have changed. Today, principles or doctrines, as they were once called, are becoming a non-issue. Every effort is being made to erase the differences that exist between the many churches that constitute Christendom. Those differences were once found in the doctrines those churches held.

Now the focus is on grace, praise, and social activity. It is suddenly inappropriate to proselytize another religion. It is as though no one is wrong anymore. The Bible has something interesting to say concerning the issue of doctrines or no doctrines in 2 Timothy 4:3, 4, "For the time will come when they will not endure sound doctrine; but after their own lusts shall they heap to themselves teachers, having itching ears; And they shall turn away their ears from the truth and shall be turned unto fables."

2 Timothy 3:5 tells of a time in the "last days" when men will have a "form of godliness but denying the power." Notice what Luke says about power in Luke 4:32, "And they were astonished at his doctrine: for his word was with power." Here Luke connects God's Word with "doctrine" and "power." Therefore, in the last days when men have a form of godliness but deny the power, can we assume that they have a religion with no doctrines or none that come from the Creator? God never changes. That which was important enough to adhere to years ago is still that important today.

Speaking of religion, there is one more aspect of the environmental movement that may have slipped by many observers. The movement is developing a very suspicious character. Not only are the religious organizations becoming more involved with the environmental movement, but the movement itself is taking on more of a religious nature.

Many involved in the movement are leading participants toward a philosophy which discourages traditional Judeo-Christian religion and encourages one of an earth-centered orientation. Religion appears to be having a profound influence on the movement as is evidenced by the previous quotations from the Earth Dialogues and Forum on Religion and Ecology at Harvard University, but the religions with the most apparent influence are the earth-centered religions.

The trend seems to hold fast here that whenever the church and the world are partnered in some endeavor rather than the church influencing the world, the church is drawn into the way of the world. This is happening in this circumstance. The result is what is called a "green religion." The appearance of the green religion is a homogenous group with few doctrines other than doing anything needed to save the earth. The focus of this religion is directed toward the earth, rather than a Supreme Being; the only commandments as Mikhail Gorbachev and Maurice Strong former U. N. Secretary say is the "Earth Charter" (2002).

This green religion will be a tolerant religion—tolerant, that is, with all but those who hold firm to a religion with principles and standards, and who worship a transcendent, loving, creator God.

"Today, one of the most powerful religions in the Western World is environmentalism," says Michael Crichton in 2003—famous author who has simultaneously held the number one book, the number one movie, and the number one TV show in the United States. He continues,

> Environmentalism seems to be the religion of choice for urban atheists. Why do I say it's a religion? Well just look at the beliefs. If you look carefully, you see that environmentalism is in fact a perfect 21st century remapping of traditional Judeo-Christian beliefs and myths.
>
> There's an initial Eden, a paradise, a state of grace and unity with nature, there's a fall from grace into a state of pollution as a result of eating from the tree of knowledge, and as a result of our actions there is a judgment day coming for us all. Sustainability is salvation in the church of the environment. Just as organic food is its communion, that pesticide-free wafer that the right people with the right beliefs, imbibe. (qtd. by Perry, 2019)

Mr. Crichton's comments, given in a speech at the Commonwealth Club in San Francisco, California, have a somewhat cynical tone because his beliefs as indicated in the speech are that "the tenants of environmentalism are all about belief. It's about whether you are going to be a sinner, or saved," he said. "Whether you are going to be one of the people on the side of salvation, or on the side of doom. Whether you are going to be one of us, or one of them."

I could not have said it better. This is what I see it all coming to. Which side are we going to be on when pressure is applied by the overwhelming majority of the world's inhabitants? When any who do not cooperate with the efforts to preserve the earth are grouped together under the heading of "fanatical fundamentalists," what will they choose? When economic sanctions are leveled against them preventing them from buying or selling unless they cooperate, what will they choose.

This is a time of great spiritual cooperation. For many years religious leaders have tried time and again to bring all the diverse faith groups together. Effort after effort have been unsuccessful. Then, along comes this "crisis" and the environmental movement that accompanied it. Suddenly all barriers have been broken down. Previous enemies are now willing to fully accept each other under the pretext of saving the earth. In other words, diabolically apposed ideologies are now working elbow to elbow.

Is it just coincidence that it's taking place now? We are in the last days! I understand that it is our tendency to put the coming of Jesus a long time in the future, but no one can deny that a time will come when He will tarry no longer. I believe that time has come. Jesus is coming! Before He does come, a test will need to be given to those who claim to be His children. The "wheat and tares" (reference) will need to be separated; His people will need to be sealed and prepared for translation. The elements are being put in place that will bring it all to pass.

The Scriptures point to a time when those who refuse to obey God will be led to "believe a lie" (2 Thess. 2:11–12).

> And then shall that Wicked be revealed, whom the Lord shall consume with the spirit of his mouth, and shall

destroy with the brightness of his coming: Even him, whose coming is after the working of Satan with all power and signs and lying wonders, And with all deceivableness of unrighteousness in them that perish; because they received not the love of the truth, that they might be saved.

And for this cause God shall send them strong delusion, that they should believe a lie: That they all might be damned who believed not the truth but had pleasure in unrighteousness. (2 Thess. 2:8–12)

Could this "crisis" we've been revealing here be that "strong delusion"? Will we be ready, or will we be swept away by the tide of public opinion and by the disguised apparently worthy cause of "saving the earth?" We must have our eyes wide open. We need to know what we believe and be ready with an answer.

CHAPTER 9

Dawning of a New World

Peace at last! The world working in harmony. Barriers of all types broken down. Finally, the whole world is realizing a problem that is greater than all the collective problems of all the nations together, and they are united in an effort toward the preservation of our planet home. Not far-fetched at all. The union is already developing. The common cause already exists. Barriers are coming down as I write. Maybe we are on the verge of the "long-expected millennium;" maybe something good is coming out of current events. Maybe we should be more optimistic about the world.

The only problem is that prophecy warns of false security and "sudden destruction." We are warned that the efforts of man fail unless they are in harmony with God's will and His plans. It matters little how well man harmonizes with his fellow man if he is not in a right relation with his Creator. The human race has been in unity since the fall. They have been united in its rebellion against the God of Creation. That's right. In this world, as apparently confused and disorderly as it appears, there is a

> *In this world, as apparently confused and disorderly as it appears, there is a harmony that remains concealed. There is unity in an all-pervasive hatred for the laws of God and a universal state of disobedience that saturates all areas of society worldwide.*

harmony that remains concealed. There is unity in an all-pervasive hatred for the laws of God and a universal state of disobedience that saturates all areas of society worldwide. To see the world uniting on an issue, is in no way a guarantee of the morality of that movement.

To the contrary, in the history of the human race there are many occasions when their unity preceded their downfall. Before the flood in Noah's day, the world was united in their rejection of Noah's message, and they were destroyed in their unity. Later at the tower of Babel they were united in constructing the tower signifying their distrust in God's promises. The tower was destroyed, languages confused, and the people scattered throughout the world.

The Bible tells us that the right way is a narrow way, and few are on it while the wrong way is a broad way (Matt. 7:13). But that is where you will find the masses. The Bible also says that the broad way is the one that leads to "destruction." It is never a good thing to feel secure merely by being with the crowd.

"Papists, Protestants, and worldling will alike accept the form of godliness without the power, and they will see in this union a grand movement for the conversion of the world and the ushering in of the long-expected millennium" (White 1972,192).

This statement reminds us that the movement for a universal Sunday law contains elements the people are convinced will usher in the "long-expected millennium." It's important to keep this in mind because the two share the same movement.

As Seventh-day Adventists, we believe in a millennium beginning after the second coming of Jesus—a time when the lost are judged. During this time Satan is on the earth, "chained" as it were because no living humans are there to be tempted and lost.

This is not the way the majority of Christians view the millennium. They see it as a time when the "saved" rule with Christ here on earth for 1,000 years. This would be a time of peace and prosperity. Because of this belief, much of the Christian world has been looking with anticipation for that time to begin.

The Scriptures describe a time just prior to the second coming that will be marked by destruction and plagues culminating with Christ appearing in the heavens. At this time the lost will be struck dead by the brightness of Christ's coming. At that time the earth will be desolate while the righteous are with God. During the thousand years the saints will be sitting on seats of judgment (2 Thess. 2:8, 1 Cor. 6:2, Matt. 19:28).

It is Satan's plan to have mankind distracted by every conceivable diversion or false doctrine, so that they will be caught unawares when this world's probation grinds to a halt. Rather than being prepared, the lost will enter into a false sense of security when they in reality are losing their grip on their only sure source of safety. At this same time they will be "crying peace and safety" (1 Thess. 5:3). While proclaiming peace and safety, then, as the scriptures say, "sudden destruction cometh upon them." That source is nothing more than trust in and obedience to the God of creation. "If you love Me, keep My commandments," Jesus says. Is it possible to be prepared to welcome Him when He returns if we don't love Him? As we just read, we cannot love Him if we are not keeping His commandments.

In the broadly expanding program for the preservation of the Earth, there is reason to believe the people will see "a grand movement for the conversion of the world and the ushering in of the long-expected millennium" (White, 1911). At the heart of this "grand movement" is the philosophy expressed in the Earth Charter whether or not the Charter itself is ever accepted universally.

The *Earth Charter* was originally drafted in 1992 at the U.N. Conference on Environment and Development (UNCED) called the Earth Summit and held in Rio de Janeiro. In the years since, the *Earth Charter* has evolved until the final version was issued on March 24th, 2000. The action plan for the convention called Earth Summit is called Agenda 21 and refers to the U.N. agenda for the 21st century.

The Preamble of the Earth Charter sets the stage for the remainder of the document. There is no need to quote the entire document; if you want to read it you can find it on the internet under *Earth Charter*. Here are a few catch words and phrases to give an example of the content:

"We stand at a critical moment in Earth's history, a time when humanity must choose its future."

"[O]ne Earth community with a common destiny. We must join together to bring forth a sustainable global society founded on respect for nature, universal human rights, economic justice, and a culture of peace" (no mention of God).

"Humanity is part of a vast evolving universe."

"The forces of nature make existence a demanding and uncertain adventure, but Earth has provided the conditions essential to life's evolution..." (The *earth* provided?)

"The choice is ours: form a global partnership to care for Earth and one another or risk the destruction of ourselves and the diversity of life. Fundamental changes are needed in our values, institutions, and ways of living..."

"We urgently need a shared vision of basic values to provide an ethical foundation for the emerging world community. Therefore, together in hope we affirm the following interdependent principles for a sustainable way of life as a common standard by which the conduct of all individuals, organizations, businesses, governments, and transnational institutions is to be guided and assessed."

Notice the references to "common destiny," "a common standard," "respect for nature," "critical moment," "evolving universe," "global partnership," "earth has provided," and "fundamental changes are needed in our values." Also see the prominence of nature, and this is just the preamble.

The remainder of the Charter lays out a plan which on the outside looks as if it would create the "millennium of peace" so long looked for by the Christian world. There are 16 principles in the remainder of the document which speak to subjects such as respect for the earth, building democratic and peaceful societies, and saving resources for future generations. There are provisions for the environment to insure its protection and its sustainable nature. This would require measures to recycle, the development of renewable energy, the elimination of all wars, and prevention of pollution in all its forms and to hold accountable those who do pollute.

The principles address lifestyles and population control, eradication of poverty, human development at all levels, and affirm gender equality; and to, "[u]phold the right of all, without discrimination, to a natural and social environment supportive of human dignity, bodily health, and spiritual well-being."

The final measures encourage the treatment with respect of all "living beings", (referring to animals) and for lifelong learning of "the skills needed for a sustainable way of life".

The last principle I would like to quote in its entirety:

a. Promote a culture of tolerance, nonviolence, and peace.
b. Encourage and support mutual understanding, solidarity, and cooperation among all peoples and within and among nations.
c. Implement comprehensive strategies to prevent violent conflict and use collaborative problem solving to manage and resolve environmental conflicts and other disputes.
d. Demilitarize national security systems to the level of a non-provocative defense posture, and convert military resources to peaceful purposes, including ecological restoration.
e. Eliminate nuclear, biological, and toxic weapons and other weapons of mass destruction.
f. Ensure that the use of orbital and outer space supports environmental protection and peace.
g. Recognize that peace is the wholeness created by right relationships with oneself, other persons, other cultures, other life, Earth, and the larger whole of which all are a part.

Can there be any better description of the "millennium of peace"? Would this not be a perfect world? Efforts are ongoing to encourage the *Earth Charter*'s acceptance by all nations. Since the Charter is fundamentally an agreement in favor of the environment, we may see rapid acceptance take place.

The Earth Charter, as I said earlier, appears to represent a mild and apparently good system for the Earth, but when studied in more depth, it reveals a system where people are willing to give up their freedoms, national sovereignty, and religious independence.

According to Maurice Strong, the Secretary General of the UNCED conference, "The real goal of the Earth Charter is that it will in fact become like the Ten Commandments" (1992). Also, Mikhail Gorbachev—last ruler of the old Soviet Union and the president of the Green Cross, a world-wide environmental organization—says this of the Earth Charter: "Do not unto the environment of others what you do not want done to your own environment...my hope is that this charter will be a kind of Ten Commandments, a 'Sermon on the Mount,' that provides a guide for human behavior toward the environment in the next century" (May 8, 1997).

Within this system, the earth becomes foremost, and belief in a Supreme being takes a lesser role if not eradicated altogether. The united world government controls the educational process, and they wish to make sure that every child is taught from an early age to relate to the earth in a new and "sacred" way. The new society will be a tolerant one as long as all are willing to comply with the new "green religion," and it will pay homage to the earth.

How can all this come to pass? To begin, the environmental movement at this time is already recognized globally. Opposition from conservative religious groups has nearly disappeared. Even the evangelical Christians are embracing the movement. Scientific consensus has come nearly completely over to the side giving the warning about "global warming." Every time a new scientific study is published about global warming the picture gets worse. The melting is found to be faster which shows the effects of warming are beginning to be felt now rather than in the future.

What makes me think that a Sabbath for the Earth will be a part of the bold new plan for earth preservation? Economics. The main reason given by many countries for not joining the Kyoto accord were economic in nature. As "reluctant governments" are convinced of the reality of the global warming crisis and convicted that something must be done, the search will be on to discover means to that end which will not be detrimental to their economies. New studies have recently been released showing that the cost of doing nothing will be greater than the cost of environmental measures themselves.

We know there will be a universally legislated Sunday law, and as already presented, there are many in the movement presently calling for a Sabbath for the Earth. Putting two and two together, I believe we will soon see an environmental Sabbath law on the books.

Another issue that we have touched on is the push toward globalization. This movement is partnered with the environmental movement. According to the prophet John in the book of Revelation, globalization is a necessity for the beast to have worldwide control. "[A]nd all the world wondered after the beast... And all that dwell upon the earth shall worship him, whose names are not written in the book of life, of the Lamb slain from the foundation of the world...And that no man might buy or sell, save he that had the mark" (Rev. 13). These verses indicate a form of globalization used by the "beast" to exercise control of the world. Here represented is a power with such universal control that economic pressure will be exerted internationally to prevent anyone from buying or selling without "worshiping" the beast.

Reading between the lines, we may also assume that the world will have a financial system which gives those in power the ability to control financial transactions worldwide. Such a system would necessarily be electronic, and most likely, it will be administered by a computer program operating through a master global data base. This has never been possible before our electronic age. This system would be very easy to establish with the World Wide Web in place today. This explains why the ruling powers today—those eager to push for world unity through the Earth Charter and the environmental movement—are also pushing the globalization movement. It would be necessary to have a unified world government to enforce the principles of this new world of peace.

There is to be a new world of peace, but it will not come by the will, hands, or laws of man. The Apostle Peter tells of what is to happen to this earth:

"But the day of the Lord will come as a thief in the night; in the which the heavens shall pass away with a great noise, and the elements shall melt with fervent heat, the earth also and the works that are therein shall be burned up…" (2 Pet. 3:10). And the Apostle John in the book of Revelation was shown in vision, "And I saw a new heaven and a new earth: for the first heaven and the first earth were passed away; and there was no more sea" (Rev. 21:1). Yes, there will be a new world; although, not the way man is expecting. Before this new world, the human race will be tested by the "beast." All will have to decide who they will follow, the Creator God, or the ways of man led by the beast who ultimately is influenced and guided by that "old serpent called the Devil" (Rev. 12:9).

This rebellious world—working to create a "sustainable" society that excludes the one true God from all its activities—is racing headlong toward a state of global denial. As the creator God is removed from the reasoning of the people, so is the Holy Spirit removed from their hearts. As this Spirit is withdrawn, the state of things will be identical to that of the people just prior to the first destruction of the world by water.

The scriptures describe that condition:

"And the LORD said, My spirit shall not always strive with man" (Gen. 6:3).

"And as it was in the days of Noe, so shall it be also in the days of the Son of man. They did eat, they drank, they married wives, they were given in marriage, until the day that Noe entered into the ark, and the flood came, and destroyed them all" (Luke 17:26–27).

"And God saw that the wickedness of man was great in the earth, and that every imagination of the thoughts of his heart was only evil continually. And it repented the LORD that he had made man on the earth, and it grieved him at his heart.And the LORD said, I will destroy man whom I have created from the face of the earth; both man, and beast, and the creeping thing, and the fowls of the air; for it repenteth me that I have made them" (Gen. 6:5–7).

The account of the flood is used by "Ecotheologists" today to represent the "first endangered species act," but the story is better suited to warn mankind of the futility of going our own way—forgetting God—and risking the loss of the restraining, refining influence of the Holy Spirit. The results at the end will be much the same as it was before the flood.

The time is coming when Jesus will make that fateful declaration, "He that is unjust, let him be unjust still: and he which is filthy, let him be filthy still: and he that is righteous, let him be righteous still: and he that is holy, let him be holy still" (Rev. 22:11). Following that event Daniel tells what is coming next: "And at that time shall Michael stand up, the great prince which standeth for the children of thy people: and there shall be a time of trouble, such as never was since there was a nation even to that same time: and at that time thy people shall be delivered, every one that shall be found written in the book" (Dan. 12:1).

> *Without doubt a new world is coming, but a world in chaos—a world in open rebellion against its Creator and unrestrained by the Spirit of God. That world will not be the utopia anticipated by many today.*

Without doubt a new world is coming, but a world in chaos—a world in open rebellion against its Creator and unrestrained by the Spirit of God. That world will not be the utopia anticipated by many today. With God's Spirit withdrawn, Satan will have complete control of those who have rejected His call of mercy. When that happens, the earth will be in a state of meltdown. Crime will be rampant and disasters most fearful will be commonplace. Cities will be destroyed, and there will be no place of safety for those who choose to obey man rather than God. *The Spirit of Prophecy* says this about that time:

> Satan works through the elements also to garner his harvest of unprepared souls. He has studied the secrets of the laboratories of nature, and he uses all his power

> to control the elements as far as God allows. When he was suffered to afflict Job, how quickly flocks and herds, servants, houses, children, were swept away, one trouble succeeding another as in a moment. It is God that shields His creatures, and hedges them in from the power of the destroyer…In accidents and calamities by sea and by land, in great conflagrations, in fierce tornadoes and terrific hailstorms, in tempests, floods, cyclones, tidal waves, and earthquakes, in every place and in a thousand forms, Satan is exercising his power. He sweeps away the ripening harvest, and famine and distress follow. (White, *The Faith I Live By*, 1958, 358)

This time—expected by some to be the beginning of the "millennium of peace" —is actually referred to by inspiration as a "time of trouble." That time is just prior to and immediately after the close of probation.

> The apostle John in vision heard a loud voice in Heaven exclaiming, 'Woe to the inhabiters of the earth and of the sea! for the devil is come down unto you, having great wrath, because he knoweth that he hath but a short time.' Revelation 12:12. Fearful are the scenes which call forth this exclamation from the heavenly voice. The wrath of Satan increases as his time grows short, and his work of deceit and destruction will reach its culmination in the time of trouble. (White, *The Great Controversy*, 1888, 623)
>
> After that time the righteous will be with the Lord for a thousand years. Then, as John foresaw, there will truly be a new heaven and a new earth: And I saw a new heaven and a new earth: for the first heaven and the first earth were passed away; and there was no more sea. And I John saw the holy city, new Jerusalem, coming down from God out of heaven, prepared as a bride adorned for her husband. And I heard a great voice out of heaven saying, Behold, the tabernacle of God is with men, and he will dwell with them, and they shall be his people, and God himself shall

be with them, and be their God. And God shall wipe away all tears from their eyes; and there shall be no more death, neither sorrow, nor crying, neither shall there be any more pain: for the former things are passed away. And he that sat upon the throne said, Behold, I make all things new. And he said unto me, write: for these words are true and faithful. (Rev. 21:1–5)

And he showed me a pure river of water of life, clear as crystal, proceeding out of the throne of God and of the Lamb. In the midst of the street of it, and on either side of the river, was there the tree of life, which bare twelve manner of fruits, and yielded her fruit every month: and the leaves of the tree were for the healing of the nations. And there shall be no more curse: but the throne of God and of the Lamb shall be in it; and his servants shall serve him. (Rev. 22:1–3)

Do not be deceived by promises of a new world of peace. The actions and agreements of men can never bring it about. No matter how wonderful it sounds, don't be deceived.

Chapter 10

A Time for Revival

What then shall we do? Do we go out into the streets with signs that read, "down with environmentalism"? Should we pack up and move to the wilderness to wait it out? No! If this theory is correct, we are in the early stages of the process. We are likely receiving an "early warning" of what is on the way. I believe there is enough evidence to warrant some action at this time. If God is giving us a glimpse into the near future, it is a merciful gift, and a space of valuable time to become better prepared for what lies ahead.

To thoroughly answer the question— "What then shall we do?" — could require more space than this entire book affords. There are entire libraries on the subject. The entire Bible could be considered an answer to the question. I have frequently drawn from the Scriptures and the published Ellen G. White writings on CD that is downloaded into my laptop. One of the hardest things about writing this book has been trying to pick a few statements out of thousands to help answer this question.

A new mindset is needed. In light of current events, we need to have a new spiritual experience.

A new mindset is needed. In light of current events, we need to have a new spiritual experience. With members of very influential organizations calling for a Sabbath for the Earth, things cannot be business as usual. What we have taken for granted must now be reevaluated and put into practice. A new spiritual reality must take possession of our being. That reality is what we have understood to be in the distant future is, in fact, right upon us.

With the apparent nearness of closing events, counsel concerning Biblical lifestyles must now be taken seriously and applied to our lives without delay. As in the day of atonement, when Israel prepared for the final transference of their sins, we need to prepare for the prospect of being without a Mediator in the Heavenly Sanctuary and for the accompanying time of trouble. There is ample reason for speedy action. "The agencies of evil are combining their forces and consolidating. They are strengthening for the last great crisis. Great changes are soon to take place in our world, and the final movements will be rapid ones" (White, *Testimonies for the Church, vol. 9,* 1909, 11).

Many are deceiving themselves by thinking that the character will be transformed at the coming of Christ, but there will be no conversion of heart at His appearing. Our defects of character must here be repented of, and through the grace of Christ we must overcome them while probation shall last. This is the place for fitting up for the family above.

"Probation is almost ended...Get ready! get ready! Work while the day lasts, for the night cometh when no man can work" (White, *God's Amazing Grace,* 1973, 243).

Rapid changes are occurring all around us. Events are transpiring that may soon cause us to be at odds with the remainder of the world. As things progress, this state of affairs will result in the laws of the land being used against us. This condition will require an experience which I feel most of us do not now possess.

This time requires a revival and a reformation. We must wake up! We are in grave danger of being deceived. The *Spirit of Prophecy* warns us that as many as half of our membership will be deceived and drawn away from our fellowship. That is difficult to accept; though, it is unlikely it can be changed. Everything must be done to warn people of the danger. This movement is likely the one to bring about this great loss. We need to have our eyes wide open concerning this issue.

"Before the final visitation of God's judgments upon the earth, there will be, among the people of the Lord, such a revival of primitive godliness as has not been witnessed since apostolic times. The Spirit and power of God will be poured out upon His children" (White, *The Faith I Live By,* 1958, 326). "A revival of true godliness among us is the greatest and most urgent of all our needs. To seek this should be our first work" (White, *Selecte Messages Book 1,* 1958, 121).

> Let us draw near with a true heart in full assurance of faith, having our hearts sprinkled from an evil conscience, and our bodies washed with pure water. Let us hold fast the profession of our faith without wavering; (for he is faithful that promised;) And let us consider one another to provoke unto love and to good works: Not forsaking the assembling of ourselves together, as the manner of some is; but exhorting one another: and so much the more, *as ye see the day approaching.* (Heb. 10:22–25)

Is this what we are experiencing here? Are we seeing the day approaching? I am firmly convinced that we are! We should follow the admonition given and see to it that we are in the fellowship of God's true obedient believers and "not forsaking the assembling of ourselves together."

> We profess to be pilgrims and strangers on earth, journeying to a better country, even an heavenly. If we are indeed but sojourners here, traveling to a land where none but the holy can dwell, we shall make it our first business to become acquainted with that country; we shall make diligent inquiry as to the preparation needed, the manners and character which we must have, in order to become citizens there. Jesus, the King of that land, is pure and holy. He has commanded his followers, "Be ye holy; for I am holy." If we are hereafter to associate with Christ and sinless angels, we must here obtain a fitness for such society.
>
> This is our work, —our all-important work. Every other consideration is of minor consequence. Our conversation, our deportment, our every act, should be such as to convince our family, our neighbors, and the world, that we expect soon to remove to a better country. More than this, our godly example should keep ever before their minds the

preparation needed by all who would enter that blessed home. Our acts must correspond with our faith, and faith will then be made perfect. We should not engage in the work of preparation merely as a duty, a necessity, but as a privilege which we are happy in accepting. Those whose faith is daily confirmed and strengthened by their works, will become acquainted with self-denial in restricting appetite, controlling ambitious desires, bringing every thought and feeling into harmony with the divine will. They will beware lest they be brought into the bondage of sin by conforming to a worldly standard, and thus, before many witnesses, denying their faith. (White, *Review and Herald,* November 29, 1881)

We, as a church, are dealing with serious conditions, within the church and without. "As the storm approaches, a large class who have professed faith in the third angel's message but have not been sanctified through obedience to the truth, abandon their position, and join the ranks of the opposition. By uniting with the world and partaking of its spirit, they have come to view matters in nearly the same light; and when the test is brought, they are prepared to choose the easy, popular side" (White, *The Faith I Live By,* 1958, 336).

During the period of delay, we have become too comfortable in this world. Unfortunately, we have permitted the world to have too much influence in our lives. Just as the children of Israel were time after time drawn into many ungodly practices by association with their idolatrous neighbors, we are also in danger of suffering consequences. There may be a lack of preparation and danger of choosing the wrong side. After knowing what we as Adventists have been privileged to know, to still be found on the wrong side when Jesus returns would be the worst nightmare I can imagine.

In light of the material presented thus far, what should our response be? Even if this interpretation were found to be an error, the response should be the same. Why? Because this scenario illustrates how easily Satan can use current events to accomplish his aims, and in so doing, deceive many. But I must repeat, the overall weight of evidence tells me that I am likely not wrong.

Review for a minute the facts presented. For a certainty Satan will do as prophesied. A Sunday law will be enacted. As to the current events surrounding the environmental movement, there could be no better event to bring about this outcome. The movement is universal and growing; there is a crisis that affects the entire globe. All the world's religions, whether Christian or Pagan, are uniting like never before, and people within the movement are already calling for a "Sabbath for the Earth." The need to combat global warming has become one of the highest priorities of most governments, and an environmental Sabbath is already in place one Sunday a year.

Continuing the review, we must remember that this scenario is compatible with the Scriptures and Spirit of Prophecy. There is mention several times in the Spirit of Prophecy of Satan working with the atmosphere "poisoning the atmosphere" and "imparting to the air a deadly taint." The Scriptures are supportive as well. Whether our preparation is geared for this crisis or another is unimportant. What is important is that we prepare.

First of all, the crisis of the last days is centered on the Sabbath, God's vs men's. In that case it would seem most appropriate that we learn all we can about the true Sabbath. Memorize all the Bible texts explaining our position. We must *know* what we believe. "But," you say, "we already know what we believe. We've studied them in Sabbath school, grade school, high school, college, and regularly in our personal devotions. What do you mean, *know* it?" We must know it inside and out. Be able to give an answer for what we believe. If the whole world is going to consider us traitors for not keeping the false Sabbath, then we will need to be firmly grounded with a strong foundation. We must live what we believe, and as the *Spirit of Prophecy* passionately pleads, we "need to be wide awake, wholly devoted, wholly converted, wholly consecrated to God" (White, Manuscript 1, 1890).

It is imperative that we study and stay informed on the issues especially those pertaining to the institution of an environmental Sabbath. If a Sunday law is instituted for the Earth it will need to be regarded as a fulfillment of prophecy since it will pay homage to the power that originally established that day as a Sabbath. Many will reason saying, "Since the law was established for non-religious reasons, why should we raise a stink bringing down the wrath of the world upon us unnecessarily?" This would be the most dangerous course to take.

When an official call comes for the establishment of a "Sabbath for the Earth" law with legislators debating the law, this would be the most opportune time to present to the world the message of the true Sabbath. At this time there are some limitations preventing public discussion of the Sabbath, but at that time the door will be wide open. Everyone will be talking about it on the TV, internet, magazines, and newspapers. This will be a time for God's people with inspiration from the Holy Spirit to give the broadest reaching Bible study on the Sabbath in the history of the church.

The experience of the children of Israel at the time of their exodus from Egypt is typical of what the remnant will have at the time of their redemption. Having lived in close proximity to the Egyptians, the Israelites for the most part had lost sight of their God and His laws. If the closeness was not a factor, the oppression and bondage by the Egyptians made it difficult to obey the Creator God. "In their bondage the Israelites had to some extent lost the knowledge of God's law, and they had departed from its precepts. The Sabbath had been generally disregarded, and the exactions of their taskmasters made its observance apparently impossible. But Moses had shown his people that *obedience to God was the first condition of deliverance*; and the efforts made to restore the observance of the Sabbath had come to the notice of their oppressors" (White, *Patriarchs and Prophets,* 1890, 258, emphasis added).

The Israelites had much to learn as well as much to unlearn. The training would continue in the wilderness where they were fed for forty years with manna from Heaven. The manna fell six days a week, and none fell on the Sabbath. None could be stored for use on another day except on Friday. Any kept until the next day would spoil. The people were told to gather enough on Friday to last them through the Sabbath, and on that occasion the manna would not spoil. Thus, the Israelites were a taught the lesson of the sacredness of the Sabbath.

This will be the experience of God's people in the last days. A message of reform will go out and the people will be called to "repair the breach" in the Sabbath, as Isaiah reminds us,

> And they that shall be of thee shall build the old waste places: thou shalt raise up the foundations of many generations; and thou shalt be called, The repairer of the breach, The restorer of paths to dwell in. If thou turn away thy foot from the Sabbath, from doing thy pleasure on my holy day; and call the Sabbath a delight, the holy of the LORD, honorable; and shalt honor him, not doing thine own ways, nor finding thine own pleasure, nor speaking thine own words: Then shalt thou delight thyself in the LORD; and I will cause thee to ride upon the high places of the earth, and feed thee with the heritage of Jacob thy father: for the mouth of the LORD hath spoken it. (Isa. 58:12–14)

As a part of the preparation needed in those days, the Sabbath will be the object of special attention since it will be the part of God's most disputed law. This will be the issue that decides the destiny of all the world.

Now, with all the information concerning a "Sabbath for the Earth" coming to light, it is time to begin the process of "repairing the breach." We need to reform our Sabbath-keeping practices. We need to learn all we can about what constitutes proper Sabbath observance and what the Sabbath is all about. How can we confront those who are keeping and attempting to enforce a false Sabbath, if we are not keeping the true Sabbath in the right spirit? Like the Israelites, if we are preparing for deliverance from this world of bondage to sin, we must be in obedience to all the Commandments of God.

At this point in time we have an opportunity to prepare for an event of this magnitude. This is why we, as a church, are here on this earth. As Mordecai said to Esther when she considered going in unannounced to talk with the king, "Who knoweth whether thou art come to the kingdom for such a time as this?" (Esther 4:14).

Again, I say, our duty is to prepare. Our duty is to study and be ready to give an answer whenever the opportunity arises. We need to know what we believe and how to explain it to others.

The Laodicean message needs to be studied and applied to our lives. We need to become familiar with its call because it is for us at this time. It is needed to prepare a people for the Second Coming. This message warns us of self-sufficiency—having a confidence in ourselves and our knowledge. This condition will lead to the very opposite outcome. Believing we don't need to learn anything new can lead to us being *unprepared*.

To feel that we possess all we need is to be "rich...and have need of nothing" (Rev. 3:17), a condition which leads to the downfall of many, even of the remnant.

"Let no man deceive himself. If any man among you seemeth to be wise in this world, let him become a fool, that he may be wise. For the wisdom of this world is foolishness with God. For it is written, He taketh the wise in their own craftiness" (1 Cor. 3:18, 19).

"Wherefore let him that thinketh he standeth take heed lest he fall" (1 Cor 10:12).

"I saw that the testimony of the True Witness has not been half heeded. The solemn testimony upon which the destiny of the church hangs has been lightly esteemed, if not entirely disregarded. This testimony must work deep repentance; all who truly receive it will obey it and be purified" (White, *Early Writings,* 1882, 270).

In the book quoted above the author describes the actions of those who are preparing for the conflict we will soon meet. Here is how she describes the event:

> I saw some, with strong faith and agonizing cries, pleading with God. Their countenances were pale and marked with deep anxiety, expressive of their internal struggle. Firmness and great earnestness was expressed in their countenances; large drops of perspiration fell from their foreheads. Evil angels crowded around, pressing darkness upon them to shut out Jesus from their view, that their eyes might be drawn to the darkness that surrounded them, and thus they be led to distrust God and murmur against Him.

The heavenly angels were continually wafting their wings over them to scatter the thick darkness...

As the praying ones continued their earnest cries, at times a ray of light from Jesus came to them, to encourage their hearts and light up their countenances. Some, I saw, did not participate in this work of agonizing and pleading. They seemed indifferent and careless. They were not resisting the darkness around them, and it shut them in like a thick cloud. The angels of God left these and went to the aid of the earnest, praying ones. I saw angels of God hasten to the assistance of all who were struggling with all their power to resist the evil angels and trying to help themselves by calling upon God with perseverance. But His angels left those who made no effort to help themselves, and I lost sight of them.

I asked the meaning of the shaking I had seen and was shown that it would be caused by the straight testimony called forth by the counsel of the True Witness to the Laodiceans. This will have its effect upon the heart of the receiver and will lead him to exalt the standard and pour forth the straight truth. Some will not bear this straight testimony. They will rise up against it, and this is what will cause a shaking among God's people. (White, *Early Writings*, 1882, 270)

This is the process we need right now to prepare a people to meet the Lord.

To the dear reader who is a Christian but may not be a Seventh-day Adventist, I make this special request: you have read the information presented in these pages. They are inspired by a sincere desire to warn all who wish to follow the Divine Shepherd; prayerfully, consider the information given here. Make use of the Appendix along with your Bible as a guide and decide for yourself what is right. The true followers of God will know truth when they see it.

Have you found yourself uncomfortable about the trends within the church you are affiliated with? Can you see the pagan influence seeping into the church? Do you miss the deep spiritual nature of worship?

The world will soon be brought to a test. The choice will be, "who do I obey? Who will I follow? Will it be the doctrines of men, or the commandments of God?" Satan, through his human instruments, has attempted to change the law of God. He is watering down the gospel to the point that nothing is important anymore. There is no right belief, for the Gospel is changed to nothing but praising God and believing. According to many church leaders, even God's commandments are no longer binding. The word of the God, who says He never changes, is changed to suit the desires of man.

Soon everyone will be in one of two groups, those who receive the mark of the beast and those who have the Seal of God. Those who receive the mark of the beast are those who have chosen to follow men, and they are led by none other than "that old serpent called the Devil," (Rev 12:9) while those who receive the Seal of God are those that hear the Shepherd's voice in His Word and follow Him.

There have always been just two ways to go as is illustrated by the "narrow" and "broad" ways in the book of Matthew. The broad way has the largest group with all their "baggage," and the narrow way has room for only those who are following the Great Shepherd. Revelation says that the whole world wondered after the beast except for the small group keeping the Commandments of God (Rev. 14:12). It's never safe to follow the crowd.

Satan's path is the broadest and the most deceptive. It is made to appear the most attractive while it is hard, mystifying, and full of disappointment. He who feels his own danger is on the watch lest he shall grieve the Holy Spirit and draw away from God. He knows that God is not pleased with his course of action. How much better and safer it is to draw nigh to God. The pure light shining from His Word may heal the wounds that sin has made in the soul. The closer we are to God, the safer we are, for Satan hates and fears the presence of God.

"The subtlety of Satan will not decrease, but the wisdom given to men through a living connection with the Source of all light and divine knowledge will be proportionate to his arts and wiles" (White, *The Faith I Live By*, 1958, 312).

Dear fellow Christians, search deeply. Let the Holy Spirit lead and be willing to go wherever He leads. Please, decide for yourself. You will be the one to pay the price since you should be the one to decide.

At this time, I would like to address former members of the Seventh-day Adventist church who have drifted away from the church for various reasons. It is time to return to the only church that teaches obedience to all the Commandments of God. At a time when the world is uniting to enforce the observance of a false Sabbath, the prophecies take on a new significance. The messages you heard when in the church regarding Sunday laws, which seemed as if they would never come, now appear to be within view. All will face trying times soon when everyone will be tested. You know this message. Please, do not find yourself trapped on the wrong side.

For those who have gone the way of a substitute body of believers feeling that the official S.D.A. church has somehow apostatized, my plea is this: come back to the body of believers. Remember, the chaff is separated from the wheat and not the other way around. God has a great work to be done by His church. We cannot do the work justice if we are separate and squabbling.

"God will have a pure church, a peculiar people, zealous of good works. He has placed the precious gifts in the church for the benefit of His people. Praise His holy name" (White, November 27, 1856).

"God's care for his heritage is unceasing. He suffers no affliction to come upon his children but such as is essential for their present and eternal good. He will purify his church, even as Christ purified the temple during his ministry on earth. All that he brings upon his people in test and trial comes that they may gain deeper piety and greater strength to carry forward the triumphs of the cross" (White, *Review and Herald,* August 8, 1912).

When Jesus purified the temple while on earth, He drove the undesirable elements out of the temple. The true believers remained.

Again, I say, The Lord hath not spoken by any messenger who calls the church that keeps the commandments of God, Babylon. True, there are tares with the wheat; but Christ said He would send His angels to first gather the tares and bind them in bundles to burn them, but gather the wheat into the garner. I know that the Lord loves His church. It is not to be disorganized or broken up into independent atoms. There is not the least consistency in this; there is not the least evidence that such a thing will be. Those who shall heed this false message and try to leaven others will be deceived and prepared to receive advanced delusions, and they will come to naught. (White, *God's Remnant Church,* 1950, 45)

"The Lord is coming. Time is short. Get ready, get ready, get ready. For Christ's sake call a halt; you have not a moment to lose. Put an end to all unjust, unrighteous criticism, and humble your hearts before God. 'Seek ye the Lord while he may be found, call ye upon him while he is near: let the wicked forsake his way, and the unrighteous man his thoughts: and let him return unto the Lord, and he will have mercy upon him; and to our God, for he will abundantly pardon'" (White, *Review and Herald,* October 31, 1893).

> *The Lord is coming. Time is short. Get ready, get ready, get ready. For Christ's sake call a halt; you have not a moment to lose.*

These are powerful statements. They cannot be ignored. Exciting things are taking place at a rapid pace! We need unity among the believers. Satan would like nothing more than to have those in the fellowship of the remnant be divided. As we prepare to give the third angel's message for the last time, we need to combine our voices. We need to give this message and the loud cry with all the volume we can muster. The call needs to be given with one voice!

When His people stand against the world, calling sin by its real name, warning the world about coming wrath, there will be those who will not endure the condemnation heaped upon us. Then they will leave our fellowship to be replaced by children of God from outside the church. Let us all join hands and create a united front against the enemy of souls.

Returning to the question, what then shall we do considering the picture that has been painted thus far in this book? I repeat a quotation from the Spirit of Prophecy, "Satan is working in the atmosphere; he is poisoning the atmosphere, and here we are dependent upon God for our lives—our present and eternal lives. And being in the position that we are, we need to be *wide awake, wholly devoted, wholly converted, wholly consecrated to God*. But we seem to sit as though we were paralyzed. God of heaven, wake us up!" (White, Manuscript 1, 1890, 52, emphasis added).

There is no place for self-sufficiency, the enemy desires to confront us "one on one" because he knows that by doing so he can win. He also desires for us to feel as though we are better off than we really are.

In the battle with our very crafty enemy, we are nothing without a close connection with our heavenly Father. This is something we cannot do halfway as the quote above from *Selected Messages* says. We cannot be partially awake, somewhat devoted, semi-converted, or a little consecrated, but our experience must be one of wholehearted effort.

> "Get ready," is the word sounded in my ears. "Get ready, get ready. He that is to come, will come and will not tarry. Tell my people that unless they improve the sacred opportunities given them, unless they do the work I have given them, Satan will come upon them *with the stealthy tread of a thief, to deceive and allure them*." God wants us to be wide awake, that when he shall come, we shall be ready to say, "Lo, this is our God; we have waited for him, and he will save us." He is coming to us by his Holy Spirit today. Let us recognize him now; then we shall recognize him when he comes in the clouds of heaven, with power

and great glory. God calls upon you to get ready to meet him in peace. (White, *Review and Herald,* April 23, 1901, emphasis added)

Satan is marshaling his host, and *are we individually prepared for the fearful conflict that is just before us? Are we preparing ourselves and our households to understand the position of our adversaries and their modes of warfare?* Are our children forming habits of decision, that they may be firm and unyielding in every matter of principle and duty? I pray that we all may understand the signs of the times, and that we may so prepare ourselves and our children that in the time of conflict God may be our refuge and defense. (White, *Child Guidance*, 555, emphasis added)

That's what this book is all about. We must know the position of our adversaries and understand their mode of warfare. I believe, as the result of this work, the mode of their warfare is becoming a little clearer.

> *"Get ready," is the word sounded in my ears. "Get ready, get ready. He that is to come, will come and will not tarry."*

Elijah had a special message for the church in his day. That message was, "Israel, get off the fence." "And Elijah came unto all the people, and said, how long halt ye between two opinions? if the LORD be God, follow him: but if Baal, then follow him. And the people answered him not a word" (1 Kings 18:21). That is my call to the people of God everywhere, get out of the neutral zone. Make a decision to yield completely to the leading of the Spirit, and give yourself unreservedly to the will of God!

John in Revelation warns of being in the lukewarm state, or middle of the road, and tells us clearly what the result will be if we stay there. Time is short, and there's no time to wait. The bundles are being gathered; the test is soon to come.

A Time for Revival

Now is the time. Now is the time for a return to "primitive Godliness" and for a "revival" (White, *The Great Controversy,* 1911). Now is a time to awake! Looking at the world around us and seeing the events taking place, we must get excited. The day is at hand! The thought that the end of all things is at the door is a most exciting prospect. To have advance warning, an urgent call, and time to prepare is an enormous blessing.

As we bring this work to a close, I would like to repeat what a trying time we face in the near future. If, the final crisis arises from a concern and an effort to save the world—especially the under privileged—we will be thrust into a most trying position. When we object to a Sunday law, we will be accused of having no concern for those suffering from climate change.

As a result, we will be linked with all the troublemakers currently plaguing the world. Our efforts to resist a Sunday law will bring down the wrath of the world on our heads. At that time, we must be solidly grounded and have faith that cannot be moved. Through the power of God alone, we will endure.

Imagine, we may be face to face with our Redeemer much sooner than we had believed. Despite the troubles we will encounter before that happens, the future could never look brighter. Finally, the long night of waiting appears to soon be over, and the dawn is about to break. What we have been waiting for is on the way. It will come. Our hopes will be realized. What we have looked for will come and is coming. Get ready, get ready, get ready!

Appendix A
The Sabbath of Creation

It is of utmost importance to understand the history of the Sabbath in order to realize the full implication of the movements taking place today. The Sabbath began at creation. Along with the weekly cycle we still have throughout the world today and all the plants and animals, the Sabbath was created that first week.

If it makes no difference what day we keep as the Sabbath this book, and the beliefs of millions of Christians around the world, would be of no importance. It is the contention of Seventh-day Adventist Christians and other believers that it does matter which day we hold sacred. This section is here to answer some of the questions on this very important subject. I will not attempt to answer every question here. Prayerfully, take your Bible and a concordance and do a thorough study into what it says about these issues.

Q. When was the Sabbath established and isn't it a Jewish custom?

A. As previously stated, the Sabbath was created with the rest of the world in the first week. "Thus the heavens and the earth were finished, and all the host of them. And on the seventh day God ended his work which he had made; and he rested on the seventh day from all his work which he had made. And God blessed the seventh day and sanctified it: because that in it he had rested from all his work which God created and made" (Gen. 2:1–3).

The Sabbath was made centuries before Abraham and his descendants. "And he said unto them, The Sabbath was made for man, and not man for the sabbath: Therefore, the Son of man is Lord also of the Sabbath" (Mark 2:27, 28). The last verse answers another question. What is the Lord's day? If Jesus is Lord of the Sabbath, (and at that time He was keeping the seventh-day Sabbath) then the Lord's day must be the Sabbath.

It is also important to realize that the commandments were in existence before they were given at Sinai, which is shown in the lessons of the manna. "And the LORD said unto Moses, how long refuse ye to keep my commandments and my laws? See, for that the LORD hath given you the sabbath, therefore he giveth you on the sixth day the bread of two days; abide ye every man in his place, let no man go out of his place on the seventh day. So the people rested on the seventh day" (Exod. 16:28–30).

The issue of observing a substitute Sabbath involves more than just the Sabbath but includes all the Commandments.

Q. Wasn't the Sabbath changed?

A. There is no scriptural authority for a change of the Sabbath. In fact, Jesus expected His people to be keeping the Sabbath many years later:

> When ye therefore shall see the abomination of desolation, spoken of by Daniel the prophet, stand in the holy place, (whoso readeth, let him understand:) Then let them which be in Judaea flee into the mountains: Let him which is on the housetop not come down to take anything out of his house: Neither let him which is in the field return back to take his clothes. And woe unto them that are with child, and to them that give suck in those days! But pray ye that your flight be not in the winter, neither on the sabbath day. (Matt. 24:15–20)

Jesus gave us an example with His life, then He said, "follow me" (Matt. 16:24). His example was, "And he came to Nazareth, where he had been brought up: and, as his custom was, he went into the synagogue on the sabbath day, and stood up for to read" (Luke 4:16).

The Sabbath was changed, but not the way many have been taught. The change was made back in the fourth century AD, according to Biblical prophecy, by the leader of the Roman church

(Daniel 7:25). This act they are more than glad to reveal because by it they claim that all other churches keeping the new Sabbath are showing homage to her. Notice this quote from *The Convert's Catechism of Catholic Doctrine* by Rev. Peter Geiermann C. SS. R:

Ques.—What is the Third Commandment?

Ans.—The Third Commandment is: Remember that thou keep holy the Sabbath day.

Ques.—Which is the Sabbath day?

Ans.—Saturday is the Sabbath day.

Ques.—Why do we observe Sunday instead of Saturday?

Ans.—We observe Sunday instead of Saturday because the Catholic Church transferred the solemnity from Saturday to Sunday.

Ques.—Why did the Catholic Church substitute Sunday for Saturday?

Ans.—The Church substituted Sunday for Saturday because Christ rose from the dead on a Sunday, and the Holy Ghost descended upon the Apostles on a Sunday.

Ques.—By what authority did the Church substitute Sunday for Saturday?

Ans.—The Church substituted Sunday for Saturday by the plentitude of that divine power which Jesus Christ bestowed upon her. (1910, 50)

Contrary to what many good, well intentioned Christians believe, many having been taught from childhood that the Apostles changed the Sabbath, the truth of the matter is that Sunday as a Sabbath is a child of the Papacy. Observe this quote from *A Doctrinal Catechism* by Stephen Keenan:

Ques.—Have you any other way of proving that the church has power to institute festivals of precept?

Ans.—Had she not such power, she could not have done that in which all modern religionists agree with her—she could not have substituted the observance of Sunday, the first day of the week, for the observance of Saturday, the seventh day, a change for which there is no Scriptural authority. (1899)

Please read one more quote about the change, this one from C. F. Thomas, Chancellor of Cardinal Gibbons, in a book entitled *Faith of our Fathers*: "Of course the Catholic Church claims that the change was her act. And the act is the mark of her ecclesiastical power and authority in religious matters" (1876). There is no Scriptural authority. We will see this quote again later in the appendix.

Q. Didn't the apostles keep Sunday as the Lord's day?

A. Many use this text in 1 Corinthians to prove that they worshiped on Sunday: "Upon the first day of the week let every one of you lay by him in store, as God hath prospered him, that there be no gatherings when I come" (1 Cor. 16:2).

Actually, it isn't proof of anything. The offerings in those days were often products of the farm and Paul did not want any gathering of crops or such to be done on the Sabbath. The fact is that in the book of Acts alone there are records of many times when the new Christian church continued to meet on the seventh-day Sabbath, often with the Gentiles, as is illustrated by the following verse:

> And when the Jews were gone out of the synagogue, the Gentiles besought that these words might be preached to them the next Sabbath. Now when the congregation was broken up, many of the Jews and religious proselytes followed Paul and Barnabas: who, speaking to them, persuaded them to continue in the grace of God. And the next Sabbath day came almost the whole city together to hear the word of God. (Acts 13:42–44)

It doesn't make sense for 1 Corinthians 16 to be how we as Christians are informed that the law of God was changed since in comparison on Mt. Sinai God's own voice and finger signaled the Law of God.. Not only that, but the Scriptures say that "God never changes" (Mal. 3:6). And that God has no intention to change His law:

> Think not that I am come to destroy the law, or the prophets: I am not come to destroy, but to fulfil. For verily I say unto you, Till heaven and earth pass, one jot or one tittle shall in no wise pass from the law, till all be fulfilled. Whosoever therefore shall break one of these least commandments, and shall teach men so, he shall be called the least in the kingdom of heaven: but whosoever shall do and teach them, the same shall be called great in the kingdom of heaven. (Matt. 5:17–19)

Some people think that this verse says that if someone breaks the Commandments they will still be in Heaven, just in a lower position. This is not so because the Bible says that sin is a transgression of the law and no one can be sinning and stand before a perfect, holy God and live.

The book of Revelation says that the people of God in the last days will be keeping the commandments of God. "Here is the patience of the saints: here are they that keep the commandments of God, and the faith of Jesus" (Rev. 14:12). Jesus said, "If ye love me, keep my commandments" (John 14:15). How can we wait anxiously for His return, expecting to see Him face to face and live eternally with Him, if we don't love Him? Satan desires to have the people believe they can be saved in their sins when in reality we must be saved from our sins. There is a difference.

Q. Does God still care if we keep Sunday or Saturday as the Sabbath?

A. Look at this verse pertaining to the people of God and the Sabbath: "And the LORD spake unto Moses, saying, Speak thou also unto the children of Israel, saying, Verily my sabbaths ye shall keep: for it is a sign between me and you throughout your generations; that ye may know that I am the LORD that doth sanctify you" (Exod. 31:12, 13). The Sabbath is not only a day to rest and worship. It is also a sign between Him and His people forever.

The scriptures tell us that in the last days there will be two marks given. One is the "mark of the beast", the other is the "seal of God". The word sign in the above text has the same meaning as seal. Those obedient to the commandments of God receive the seal, while those who choose to disregard the commands of God, receive the mark of the beast. The sign or seal help us to "remember" (Exod. 20:8) who our God is, and that we are dependent on Him for our sanctification.

Q. What day will be the Sabbath after Jesus returns?

A. "For as the new heavens and the new earth, which I will make, shall remain before me, saith the LORD, so shall your seed and your name remain. And it shall come to pass, [that] from one new moon to another, and from one sabbath to another, shall all flesh come to worship before me, saith the LORD" (Isa. 66:22, 23). At the time of Isaiah there was only one Sabbath and it is clear that the context of this verse is after Jesus returns. There is no doubt that we will be worshiping the Lord of the Sabbath on the Sabbath day He created.

Appendix B

The Mark of the Beast

In this section we will begin to see why it is so important to know which is the true Sabbath.

Q. Who or what is the beast?

A. We will go directly to Revelation chapter 13 for our first look at the beast:

> And I stood upon the sand of the sea, and saw a beast rise up out of the sea, having seven heads and ten horns, and upon his horns ten crowns, and upon his heads the name of blasphemy. And the beast which I saw was like unto a leopard, and his feet were as the feet of a bear, and his mouth as the mouth of a lion: and the dragon gave him his power, and his seat, and great authority. And I saw one of his heads as it were wounded to death; and his deadly wound was healed: and all the world wondered after the beast. And they worshipped the dragon which gave power unto the beast: and they worshipped the beast, saying, Who [is] like unto the beast? who is able to make war with him? And there was given unto him a mouth speaking great things and blasphemies; and power was given unto him to continue forty and two months. And he opened his mouth in blasphemy against God, to blaspheme his name, and his tabernacle, and them that dwell in heaven. And it was given unto him to make war with the saints, and to overcome them: and power was given him over all

kindreds, and tongues, and nations. And all that dwell upon the earth shall worship him, whose names are not written in the book of life of the Lamb slain from the foundation of the world. If any man have an ear, let him hear. He that leadeth into captivity shall go into captivity: he that killeth with the sword must be killed with the sword. Here is the patience and the faith of the saints. (Rev. 13:1–10)

This same power is mentioned in the book of Daniel also:

I considered the horns, and, behold, there came up among them another little horn, before whom there were three of the first horns plucked up by the roots: and, behold, in this horn were eyes like the eyes of man, and a mouth speaking great things. Then I would know the truth of the fourth beast, which was diverse from all the others, exceeding dreadful, whose teeth were of iron, and his nails of brass; which devoured, brake in pieces, and stamped the residue with his feet; And of the ten horns that were in his head, and of the other which came up, and before whom three fell; even of that horn that had eyes, and a mouth that spake very great things, whose look was more stout than his fellows. I beheld, and the same horn made war with the saints, and prevailed against them; Until the Ancient of days came, and judgment was given to the saints of the most High; and the time came that the saints possessed the kingdom. Thus, he said, the fourth beast shall be the fourth kingdom upon earth, which shall be diverse from all kingdoms, and shall devour the whole earth, and shall tread it down, and break it in pieces. And the ten horns out of this kingdom are ten kings [that] shall arise: and another shall rise after them; and he shall be diverse from the first, and he shall subdue three kings. And he shall speak great words against the most High, and shall wear out the saints of the most High, and think to change times and laws: and they shall be given into his hand until a time and times and the dividing of time. (Dan. 7:8, 19–25)

An angel explains the images to Daniel. The beasts he saw were kingdoms, beginning at his time and going to the end of the world. The horns were kings that would rule in the time period of that beast power. The little horn was a power that would arise and uproot three other kings in the process. That little horn represents the Papacy.

The last beast with the ten horns was the Roman Empire, which eventually dissolved into ten smaller kingdoms. The Papacy received a throne from the Roman Emperor and as his throne was established three of the ten kingdoms were removed, as prophesied.

The horn representing the Papacy was to blaspheme God, think to change "times and laws," and persecute the saints of God for "time and times and the dividing of time" (Dan. 7:25). Converting this time period using ancient methods turns the *time* into a year, with *times* being two years, and the *dividing of time* being one half year. Changing the three and a half years into days we have 1260 days, and a day in prophecy is equal to a year. Therefore, the horn would persecute the saints for 1260 years.

As we have already seen, the Papacy persecuted the people of God for 1260 years before the Pope was taken captive by a French general in 1798. Another part of the prophecy of the little horn is his thinking to change times and laws. This was accomplished when the Pope rewrote the Ten Commandments, removing the second about worshiping idols, and changing the Sabbath from Saturday to Sunday as we have already discussed.

The little horn would blaspheme God. The Biblical description for blaspheme is for a man to claim to forgive sins, and for a man to claim to be God (Mark 2:7; John 10:33). These two things the Papacy is guilty of. The Pope claims to be God on earth, and the priests claim to be able to forgive sins.

Now let's take all this information and look at the beast in Revelation 13. We see a beast coming up out of the sea, which represents nations and tongues and peoples. The beast appears to be a conglomeration of all four beasts in Daniel 7. The dragon gave him his seat and power and great authority. At the time of Christ, the Roman Empire was the power used by the dragon (Satan). This same beast was to blaspheme God and make war with the saints. The time period appears to be different, though. Looking at the time, we find that forty and two months is equal to 1260 days. A day for a year means that this power was to continue for 1260 years. Beginning at the time the Papacy was established to the time he was taken into captivity was exactly 1260 years.

The prophecy in Revelation says that the beast would receive a deadly wound, but that the deadly wound would be healed. The prophecy also said the beast would go into captivity. In 1798 the Pope was taken into captivity by the French general Berthier. While captive he eventually became ill and died. To all observers it would seem that the Papacy was dead also. But with time the wound was healed and the Papacy has regained all, if not more, than it once had. The world once again appears to be taken with the colorful, charismatic personality of the Pontiff of Rome.

Q. What about the number 666?

A. Let's read what Revelation says about the number. "Here is wisdom. Let him that hath understanding count the number of the beast: for it is the number of a man; and his number is Six hundred threescore and six" (Rev. 13:18). In Bible times it was a custom to change a person's name into a number. Let's play around with the Pope's name and see what we get. The Pope has a crown with the words *Vicarius Filii Dei*, which is Latin for Vicar of the Son of God. If we convert all the letters that are Roman numerals and add them, let's see what number we get.

V	5	F	No value	D	500
I	1	I	1	E	No value
C	100	L	50	I	1
A	No value	I	1		
R	No value	I	1		
I	1				
U/V	5				
S	No value				
	=112		=53		=501
112+53+501=666					

Yes, just as you probably guessed, the numbers add up to 666. Interesting, isn't it? There are many other reasons that the number 666 is associated with the beast, some pagan in origin dating back to ancient Babylon. If you are not a Seventh-day Adventist, you may want to contact the local Seventh-day Adventist pastor to get more information on the number and other characteristics of the beast.

Q. The evidence seems quite convincing, but what is the mark?

A. We need to go back and review some of the characteristics of the beast. The beast is a blasphemous religious system which sets man at a level with God. The beast is also responsible for attempting to change the law of God by changing the Sabbath from the original Saturday to Sunday, the original "venerable day of the sun".

In order to see how this all applies, let's go back and look again at a quote used earlier from C. F. Thomas, Chancellor of Cardinal Gibbons, in a book entitled *Faith of our Fathers*. "Of course the Catholic Church claims that the change was her act. And the act is *the mark of her ecclesiastical power and authority in religious matters*" (1895, emphasis added).

The mark of the organization which scholars from many religions have thought for years to be the beast of Revelation, according to their own words, is the change of the Sabbath. The establishment of a false Sabbath, one set up by man for man's convenience and for the glory of the Papacy in flagrant opposition to the King of the universe, is the root of the mark of the beast.

As I mentioned in the main body of the book, no one receives the mark of the beast until the false Sabbath is forced by law and everyone will have to decide whether they will obey God or man. Then and only then will someone receive the mark. I believe that what the material I have presented is telling us is that the time for this to take place is not far in the future. We may already be able to see the first movement in that direction.

The Scriptures reveal that the whole world wondered after the beast. Will we soon see a global environmental Sabbath for the Earth? If accepted by the world it would constitute the world paying homage to the power that originally made that day a Sabbath. We must be prepared.

Appendix C

The Spirit of Prophecy

And it shall come to pass afterward, that I will pour out my spirit upon all flesh; and your sons and your daughters shall prophecy, your old men shall dream dreams, your young men shall see visions: and also upon the servants and upon the handmaids in those days will I pour out my spirit. (Joel 2:28, 29)

This was the verse quoted by Paul as recorded in Acts 2: 17, 18, which he repeated to explain what was happening on the day of Pentecost. But this was not the only time the prophecy in Joel was to be fulfilled. If it was important enough for God to send messages at the beginning of the Gospel dispensation, would it not surely be needed as much at the end of the period?

God promised to send the "rain" of the Holy Spirit, the "early" and the "latter" rain (Joel 2:23; James 5:7). The early rain came on Pentecost and has been present with us ever since. How we respond to it determines whether we will receive a greater outpouring. If we are not making use of the early rain, we will never have part in the latter rain!

When God pours out His Spirit, those receiving it are capable of all manner of miracles, including prophecy. God's last-day people will have the gift of prophecy according to the book of Revelation:

"And the dragon was wroth with the woman and went to make war with *the remnant of her seed, which keep the commandments of God, and have the testimony of Jesus Christ.*" "And I fell at his feet to worship him. And he said unto me, see thou do it not: I am thy fellow servant, and of thy brethren that have the testimony of Jesus: worship God: for *the testimony of Jesus is the spirit of prophecy*" (Rev. 12:17; 19:10, emphasis added). They not only have the "Spirit of Prophecy," but also "keep the commandments of God." We, in the Seventh-day Adventist Church, feel that God has given us the gift of prophecy in one of our early founders.

That person was Ellen G. White, born Ellen Harmon on November 26, 1827, in Gorham, Maine. At the age of 9, Ellen was seriously injured by a blow to her face from a rock thrown by an angry child. Ellen nearly died. She describes her ordeal in her own words:

> I have no recollection of anything further for some time after the accident. My mother said that I noticed nothing but lay in a stupor for three weeks. No one but herself thought it possible for me to recover, but for some reason she felt that I would live.
>
> When I again aroused to consciousness, it seemed to me that I had been asleep. I did not remember the accident, and was ignorant of the cause of my illness. A great cradle had been made for me, and in it I lay for many weeks. I was reduced almost to a skeleton.
>
> At this time, I began to pray the Lord to prepare me for death. When Christian friends visited the family, they would ask my mother if she had talked with me about dying. I overheard this, and it roused me. I desired to become a Christian and prayed earnestly for the forgiveness of my sins. I felt a peace of mind resulting, and loved everyone, feeling desirous that all should have their sins forgiven, and love Jesus as I did. (White, *Life Sketches,* 1915, 17, 18)

Ellen's wounds slowly healed, though she remained chronically ill for some time. Because of the injury Ellen was not able to continue school with the other children. She basically had to learn to write anew. The remainder of her education was essentially self-taught, with God's help.

Appendix C: The Spirit of Prophecy | 151

At the age of 12, Ellen was baptized into the Methodist Church. In March of 1840 William Miller was in Portland, Maine, to give lectures on the Second Coming of Christ. Ellen and some friends attended the meetings. Of these meetings she had this to say:

> Mr. Miller traced down the prophecies with an exactness that struck conviction to the hearts of his hearers. He dwelt upon the prophetic periods and brought many proofs to strengthen his position. Then his solemn and powerful appeals and admonitions to those who were unprepared, held the crowds as if spellbound.
>
> I had been taught that a temporal millennium would take place prior to the coming of Christ in the clouds of heaven; but now I was listening to the startling announcement that Christ was coming in 1843, only a few short years in the future.
>
> Special meetings were appointed where sinners might have an opportunity to seek their Savior and prepare for the fearful events soon to take place. Terror and conviction spread through the entire city. Prayer meetings were established, and there was a general awakening among the various denominations; for they all felt more or less the influence that proceeded from the teaching of the near coming of Christ. (White, *Life Sketches,* 1915, 20, 21)

Ellen followed the advent meetings for several years. When she was 17, while in a prayer meeting with friends, she had her first vision. She describes the event that would be the first of thousands of such occasions: "[A]t this time, I visited one of our Advent sisters, and in the morning, we bowed around the family altar. It was not an exciting occasion, and there were but five of us present, all women. While I was praying, the power of God came upon me as I had never felt it before. I was wrapped in a vision of God's glory, and seemed to be rising higher and higher from the earth, and was shown something of the travels of the Advent people to the Holy City" (White, *Early Writings,* 1882, 11, 12).

The messages she received over the years contained instructions about Christian living in addition to light on events from Bible times, historical references to prophetic events, health principles, personal admonition to individuals, and prophecies of last day events such as those used in this book (often referred to as the *Spirit of Prophecy*). She was clear on the position her writings were to hold in connection with the Scriptures. Her work was always to be considered a "lesser light" (White, *Testimonies for the Church, vol. 8,* 1904). Her messages, according to the test of a true prophet in Scripture, have always been shown to harmonize with God's word. In her writings she is repeatedly referring the reader to the Scriptures. And unlike the average prophet today, her prophecies have come to pass as predicted.

The Ellen G. White writings have spoken with spiritual effectiveness to people of many cultures and languages. *Steps to Christ* has been translated into 117 different languages, making Ellen G. White "the fourth most-translated author in the history of literature, its most-translated woman writer, and the most translated American author of either sex" (Coon, in Maxwell, *God Cares,* vol. 2, 1985, 21).

> At her death in 1915 the editor of New York City *Independent* said of her, "She showed no spiritual pride and she sought no filthy lucre. She lived the life and did the work of a worthy prophetess" (1915). In the 1950s William Foxwell Albright, the renowned archaeologist who wrote over 800 articles and was awarded 25 honorary doctorates, investigated Ellen White and pronounced her an authentic prophet. Her philosophy of education, as expressed in her book *Education,* has been published with resounding praise by the government of Japan. Her instructions for better health—so strange when she wrote them, so normal today—have been praised by various experts. (Maxwell, 405, 406)

The Bible says that "by their fruits ye shall know them" (Matt. 7:20), and those words could be no truer of Ellen White. Her work and her life testified unmistakably to the source of her messages. The lives affected and the light given were all from a woman who because of a serious injury was not expected to live.

The best way to test her inspiration is to read her books and see for yourself. We as Seventh-day Adventists believe she was Divinely inspired, and in that light, we believe that her views into the future end time events are of too serious a nature to be lightly disregarded.

Bibliography

Bacchiocchi, Samuele. *Divine Rest for Human Restlessness: A Theological Study of the Good News of the Sabbath for Today.* Biblical Perspectives, 1998.

Bansen, Geoff. "What Is COVID-19's Effect on the Environment?" News 12, April 3, 2020. https://1ref.us/1gu (accessed December 10, 2020).

Bassett, Libby, Kusumita P. Pedersen, and John T. Brinkman. *Earth and Faith: A Book of Reflection for Action.* UN Environment Programme, 2000.

Brockhaus, Hannah. "Vatican to Mark 5th Anniversary of Laudato Si' with Year-Long Celebration." Catholic News Agency, May 19, 2020. https://1ref.us/1gv (accessed December 10, 2020).

Callicott, J. Baird. "Environmental Ethics: An Overview." Yale Forum on Religion and Ecology (2000). https://1ref.us/1gw (accessed December 16, 2020).

Chartres, Rev. Dr. Richard, bishop of London. Audio Lectures. Gresham College. https://1ref.us/1h9 (accessed December 7, 2020).

Crittendon, Guy. "The New IPCC Report on Climate Change." Blog (February 2, 2007). https://1ref.us/1gx (accessed December 7, 2020).

Doyle, Alister. "Rising Oceans Could Threaten Low-Lying Coasts." Reuters, December 14, 2006. https://1ref.us/1gy (accessed December 16, 2020).

Earth Bible: Reading the Bible from the Perspective of the Earth. https://1ref.us/1gz (accessed December 16, 2020).

Earth Charter Dialogues. 2002. https://1ref.us/1h0 (accessed December 16, 2020).

Geiermann, C. SS. R Rev. Peter. *The Convert's Catechism of Catholic Doctrine*. St. Louis: B. Herder Book Co., 1930.

Gibbons, James Cardinal. *Faith of Our Fathers*. New York: John Murphy & Company, 1876.

"God's Earth Is Sacred." National Council of Churches. 2005. https://1ref.us/1gt (accessed December 16, 2020).

Gottlieb, Roger S., ed. *This Sacred Earth: Religion, Nature, Environment*, 2nd edition. New York: Routledge, 2004. https://1ref.us/1h1 (accessed December 16, 2020).

Sagan, Dr. Carl. "An Open Letter to the Religious Community." Global Forum of Spiritual and Parliamentary Leaders Conference, Moscow, Russia, 1990. https://1ref.us/1h2 (accessed November 19, 2020).

"Be Worried. Be Very Worried." *Time* 167, no. 14 (April 3, 2006).

Intergovernmental Panel on Climate Change (IPCC). *Climate Change 2007: Impacts, Adaptation and Vulnerability*. New York: Cambridge University Press, 2007. https://1ref.us/1h3 (accessed November 19, 2020).

Keenan, Stephen. *A Doctrinal Catechism*. New York: P.J. Kennedy, 1899.

Kluger, Jeffrey. "Environment: Why Are These Frogs Croaking?" *TIME Magazine,* January 23, 2006. https://1ref.us/1h4 (accessed December 16, 2020).

Maxwell, C. Mervyn. *God Cares Volume 2: The Message of Revelation*. Nampa, ID: Pacific Press, 1985.

National Religious Partnership for the Environment and the Union of Concerned Scientists. *Keeping the Earth: Religious and Scientific Perspectives on the Environment*. 1996. https://1ref.us/1h5 (accessed November 19, 2020).

Perry, Mark J. "Michael Crichton in 2003: Environmentalism Is a Religion." *AEIdeas* (April 17, 2019). https://1ref.us/1h6 (accessed December 16, 2020).

Pope Francis. *Laudato Si'*. Encyclical. May 24, 2015. https://1ref.us/1h7 (accessed December 10, 2020).

Rios, Jill. "Back to the Garden: Cultivating Environmental Advocacy in the Christian South." Southern Environmental Law Center, 2006.

Randall, R. Mitch. "Ecological Responsibility." Christians for Change Blog (March 17, 2005). https://1ref.us/1h8 (accessed December 10, 2020).

Schade, Leah D. "When Earth Demands Sabbath: Learning from the Coronavirus Pandemic." EcoPreacher (April 1, 2020). https://1ref.us/1ha (accessed December 10, 2020).

Sherwood, Diane. "Ecology and the Church: Theology and Action." *The Christian Century* (May 13, 1987). https://1ref.us/1hb (accessed December 16, 2020).

Sleeth, Matthew. "The Future of Eco-Evangelism." Blessed Earth. April 23, 2005. https://1ref.us/1hc (accessed December 10, 2020).

Tucker, Mary, and John Grim. "The Challenge of the Environmental Crisis." Center for the Study of World Religions, Harvard Divinity School, 1997. https://1ref.us/1hd (accessed December 16, 2020).

UN Environmental Programme. "Only One Earth." The United Nations Environmental Sabbath Service. New York, 1990. https://1ref.us/1he (accessed November 19, 2020).

"Warming Expert: Only Decade Left to Act in Time." MSNBC News Service, September 14, 2006. https://1ref.us/1hf (accessed December 7, 2020).

White, Ellen G. *Child Guidance.* Washington, DC: Review and Herald Publishing Association, 1954.

———. *Counsels for the Church*. Nampa, ID: Pacific Press Publishing Association, 1991.

———. *Counsels from the Spirit of Prophecy on Labor Unions and Confederacies.* Silver Spring, MD: General Conference of Seventh-day Adventists, 1969.

———. *Early Writings.* Washington, DC: Review and Herald Publishing Association, 1882.

———. *The Faith I Live By.* Washington, DC: Review and Herald Publishing Association, 1958.

———. *Fundamentals of Christian Education.* Nashville, TN: Southern Publishing Association, 1923.

———. *God's Remnant Church.* Mountain View, CA: Pacific Press Publishing Association, 1950.

———. *The Great Controversy.* Mountain View, CA: Pacific Press Publishing Association, 1911.

———. *The Great Controversy (1888 Edition).* Mountain View, CA: Pacific Press Publishing Association, 1888.

———. *Last Day Events.* Boise, ID: Pacific Press Publishing Association, 1992.

———. *Life Sketches of Ellen G. White.* Mountain View, CA: Pacific Press Publishing Association, 1915.

———. *Maranatha.* Washington, DC: Review and Herald Publishing Association, 1976.

———. *The Ministry of Healing.* Mountain View, CA: Pacific Press Publishing Association, 1905.

———. *Patriarchs and Prophets.* Washington, DC: Review and Herald Publishing Association, 1890.

———. *Selected Messages.* Book 1. Washington, DC: Review and Herald Publishing Association, 1958.

———. *Selected Messages.* Book 2. Washington, DC: Review and Herald Publishing Association, 1958.

———. *Selected Messages.* Book 3. Washington, DC: Review and Herald Publishing Association, 1980.

———. *The SDA Bible Commentary.* Vol. 7A. Washington, DC: Review and Herald Publishing Association, 1970.

———. *The Spirit of Prophecy.* Vol. 4. Battle Creek, MI: Seventh-day Adventist Publishing Association, 1884.

———. *Testimonies for the Church.* Vol. 6. Mountain View, CA: Pacific Press Publishing Association, 1901.

———. *Testimonies for the Church*. Vol. 8. Mountain View, CA: Pacific Press Publishing Association, 1904.

———. *Testimonies for the Church*. Vol. 9. Mountain View, CA: Pacific Press Publishing Association, 1909.

White, Lynn Jr. "The Historical Roots of Our Ecologic Crisis." *Science,* New Series, Vol. 155, No. 3767 (Mar. 10, 1967). https://1ref.us/1hg (accessed December 16, 2020).

TEACH Services, Inc.
P U B L I S H I N G

We invite you to view the complete
selection of titles we publish at:
www.TEACHServices.com

We encourage you to write us
with your thoughts about this,
or any other book we publish at:
info@TEACHServices.com

TEACH Services' titles may be purchased in
bulk quantities for educational, fund-raising,
business, or promotional use.
bulksales@TEACHServices.com

Finally, if you are interested in seeing
your own book in print, please contact us at:
publishing@TEACHServices.com
We are happy to review your manuscript at no charge.

www.ingramcontent.com/pod-product-compliance
Lightning Source LLC
Chambersburg PA
CBHW071609170426
43196CB00034B/2244